LEADERSHIP ATTRIBUTES *for* WOMEN *and* MEN

. . . .

Leading Community in Disruptive Times

*We have a your ... a
to share
wonderful journey*

Love a Blessings

Vicky

Visit Vicky's website to download your **free journal** to record your thoughts and reflections as you read this book (the journal includes mandalas to colour in).

www.vickymcgahey.com

Also available at the website are other helpful resources including **The Leadership Attributes Game**.

LEADERSHIP ATTRIBUTES *for* WOMEN *and* MEN

. . . .

Leading Community in Disruptive Times

Dr VICKY McGAHEY

First published 2016 by
Vicky McGahey

www.vickymcgahey.com

©Vicky McGahey

This book is copyright. Except for private study research, criticism or reviews, as permitted under the Copyright Act, no part of this book may be reproduced, stored in a retrieval system or transmitted in any form or by any means without prior written permission. Enquiries should be made to the publisher.

Editor: Janet Parker
Designer: Stan Lamond
Proofreader: Brian Mayne

Printed in Australia

National Library of Australia Cataloguing-in-Publication Data
Creator: McGahey, Vicky, author.
Title: Leadership attributes for women and men : leading
    community in disruptive times / Vicky McGahey.
ISBN: 9780994467904 (paperback)
Notes: Includes index.
Subjects: Leadership.
          Community leadership.
          Executive coaching.
          Executive ability.
Dewey Number: 658.4092

ISBN 978-0-9944679-0-4 (softcover)
ISBN 978-0-9944679-1-1 (e-book)

For

Those who search within themselves
for happiness and peace

My mum

Contents

About the Author 8
Acknowledgments. 9

Introduction 11

Part 1	**Leadership: Simple Reflections**. 17	
Chapter 1	Leaders are Born or Leaders are Made? 18	
Chapter 2	'Becoming' 36	
Part 2	**The Leadership Attributes** 49	
Chapter 3	The Model of the Leadership Attributes 50	
Chapter 4	INTEGRITY – Trust – Trustworthy 54	
Chapter 5	PROPHECY – Transcendence – Faith 75	
Chapter 6	EMPATHY – Compassion – Passion. 95	
Chapter 7	INTUITION – Risk. 118	
Chapter 8	JUDGMENT – Diversity 137	
Chapter 9	COMMUNICATION – Consistency. 152	
Chapter 10	The Leadership Attributes in Action 168	
Chapter 11	Summary and Conclusion 174	
Appendix A	The Leadership Attributes 180	
Appendix B	The Conceptual Theories of the Leadership Attributes Study. 186	
Appendix C	The Shepherd Metaphor 197	
Appendix D	*The Invitation* by Oriah Mountain Dreamer. 204	
Appendix E	Benjamin Franklin's 13 Virtues. 207	

Endnotes 208
Index 218
Additional Information 223

About the Author

Vicky McGahey was born in Perth, Western Australia. She has lived in Sydney for most of her life and has worked as a teacher, entertainer, speaker and lecturer. Vicky has a doctorate degree and several masters degrees, including one in Theology. Her doctorate focused on the subject of leadership and the attributes required to be a good and moral leader. Vicky is a high school teacher of religion, science and music. She has held several head teacher roles including Director of Human Resources.

Vicky is also the author of a Young Adult series titled *The Kingdom of Wizards*. The series features fantasy stories, each founded in reality and filled with mystery and adventure. The stories teach the young mind that the ability to lead lies within us all.

Vicky is an accomplished singer and a songwriter who is also a keynote speaker and presenter. As an active member of the community, her interests include politics, leadership theory and practice, theology, the Australian bush, scuba diving, self-reflection, writing and the study of the voice.

Acknowledgments

The writing of this book is another step in a continuing journey that has been shared with many people along the way. This includes the participants in the Leadership Attributes Study that formed part of my doctorate research, the students of the Australian Catholic University (ACU) in the field of educational leadership and the children I have taught as a secondary school teacher.

This book would not have begun without the inspiration, guidance and gift that is Matt Church. It would never have been completed without the critique, support and work of three people: Janet Parker, the ever-patient, knowledgeable and kind editor from whom I have learnt so much; Stan Lamond, who creatively and insightfully provided the graphics and overall design; and Brian Mayne, without whom the journey towards 'becoming' a writer would never have evolved. Brian's creative editorial ability and belief in this work is a constant guiding force. I am grateful for his gift of time and the wonderful hours shared in making this and other works a reality.

Acknowledgment to significant others includes Dr Barry Harris, my doctorate supervisor, who first critiqued the Leadership Attributes; colleagues at ACU for the opportunity to develop and share the attributes in our work; and the community that is Mater Maria Catholic College, who display the attributes beautifully and most fully in the lives they lead with our students. You are a source of inspiration and hope.

Special thanks to my mother, who remains my source of love and is my greatest fan, and to my friends, many of whom have listened patiently and then thought to themselves: 'She's off again.'

To you, the readers, I hope you come to realise that leadership is service. To do it well you need to lead with grace. Leadership is not a position, leadership is a choice. And once chosen, leadership is a journey that has no ending … so let your Leadership Attributes shine.

Introduction

Sensing Camelot

I have never regarded myself as someone who seeks perfection, but the reality is that deep down I do. This underlying need has led me on a grail-like quest to find the foundation stones for building a Camelot. Famed in Arthurian legend, Camelot is a mythical place where all are considered equal, decision-making is shared through open dialogue and all voices are heard. In the words of Sean Connery's King Arthur of Camelot in the movie *First Knight*, as he assembled the Knights of the Round Table:

> May God grant us the wisdom to discover the right
> The willingness to choose it
> and the strength to make it endure
> **(Lowry & Zucker, 1995)**[1]

This yearning started to emerge while clinging to the rail of a ship heading for sheltered waters during a raging storm (the worst ever recorded in the Mediterranean in the 1980s). It is amazing what 24 hours of seasickness can do to a person's body, mind and soul! I was working as a solo female entertainer on board the luxury ship MV *Orient Express* (yes, the big sister to the famous train) during 1987. The wide blueness of the ocean and its changing moods has long been the source of inspiration for poets and musicians. The months at sea, with its endless 'waters moving beneath my feet' experiences, stimulated the birth of a dream: the establishment of a Specialist Music School (SMS), located in the western suburbs of Sydney, for talented and gifted young musicians. Unfortunately, the school was not to be. Though it did achieve general recurrent funding from the Australian

Government of $5 million over 3 years, along with the go-ahead from the necessary organisational bodies, the start-up requirements of student numbers and other secured funds made it unfeasible. So it remains an unfulfilled dream for now.

At the time, I did not realise the true purpose of this yearning, which was the need to establish a caring and nurturing community … a Camelot … a community that erred on the side of goodness and goodwill. The realisation of this purpose occurred many years later, while trying to splice together various areas of study as I worked on my doctorate. The findings of two research studies (1993–2000) – including an extensive literature review and the storyteller nature of that work – has stood the test of time. Not much has changed in the field of leadership. There is still the need for leadership and learning to be transformational so that good (moral) communities can emerge.

My experiences and my reflections on those experiences caused a change and growth within me. I have undergone a number of transformative learning experiences that have been a significant disruption and challenge to my thinking and my way of doing things. In simple terms, transformative learning is a shift in thinking that can change one's actions. It signifies a movement to a new knowing and a new outlook on the way things can or cannot be done. Transformative learning is one of the foundation stones upon which this book rests. The others are transformational leadership and moral community. I have defined a moral community as 'a community that values the heart, soul and mind of its people through the growth and development of shared principles, values and beliefs.'[2]

Transformational leadership is a style of leadership where the leader manages meaning, creates vision and empowers others towards becoming self-leaders. This perspective assumes leadership potential in everyone.[3]

With this in mind, I could not, with all due respect, neglect to mention the plight of women in leadership. There is a significant gender imbalance within many walks of life at present, but especially in leadership roles within organisations, government, politics, local groups and, often, the family. There seems to be an acceptance within society that women should not be in leadership roles – that a woman's place is in the home or doing the more menial tasks – and that we should leave the men in charge. Quite sad and very limiting and not truly celebratory of the gifts and talents women can bring to leadership per se. Yes, there are a chosen few who have broken through the barriers (the glass ceiling), however, I feel there are people who merely tolerate women in leadership roles because, at best, it is seen as the right thing to do by male and, sadly, other female counterparts. Also, there are women in leadership roles that are more 'behind the scenes'. These women leaders are not so visible or in the public eye. This reality continues to have a detrimental effect upon the potential growth of a just and moral society. The world suffers because of gender imbalance.

You have to ask yourself why this state of affairs, this gender imbalance in so many fields, continues to exist and is perpetuated. Why? Why? Why? The answer is simple! Conditioning … hundreds of years of conditioning!

I was told that a 'problem is only a solution waiting to be found'. This problem deserves serious consideration by every one of us as we face the onslaught of fundamentalism – be it religious, cultural or political. There is a need for leadership that transforms humanity through tolerance, authenticity and respect. In this way, good and moral communities – ones that encourage learning and sustainable growth – can be built. Such growth also requires a balance between all things, such as desires, needs and gender. Sadly, as previously stated, there is a lack of female representation in leadership roles within our world. Within the pages of this book are the stories of both men and women who, in their own way, were leaders of their time.

Part 1 discusses the very fluid concept of leadership (Chapter 1). Hopefully, this will establish a reason or purpose to continue to read and reflect upon what is needed to 'become' (Chapter 2).

Part 2 presents the Leadership Attributes, which are the main focus of this book (Chapters 3–9). It describes the Leadership Attributes as a call to action, with a strategy for implementation (Chapter 10). In this way, a sustainable community can be built (Chapter 11).

It is important to note that when the word 'community' is used in this book, it means community within an organisation, including not-for-profit organisations like Rotary; local groups; in the family; or in any setting where two or more people gather together. The formation of a community rests at the heart of leadership. You are not a leader without followers and a leader needs to nurture and foster relationships that build community.

Appendices A–E provide in-depth references to and descriptions of the concepts presented in the chapters, and each appendix is cross-referenced where appropriate. The appendices are as follows:

- Appendix A   The Leadership Attributes
- Appendix B   The Conceptual Theories of the Leadership Attributes Study
- Appendix C   The Shepherd Metaphor
- Appendix D   *The Invitation*, by Oriah Mountain Dreamer
- Appendix E   Benjamin Franklin's 13 Virtues

The Leadership Attributes (Appendix A) are the qualities that lie within each and every one of us. They are given a voice through our words and brought to life through our actions. The attributes can help to make every human life one of purpose, service and fulfilment. An eight-year study uncovered 15 Leadership Attributes.[4] These are discussed more fully in Part 2.

Appendix B presents several of the conceptual theories underpinning the work that led to the formation of the Leadership Attributes – the main topic of this book. These are *learning*, *leadership* and *community*. Both learning and leadership are seen as needing to be transformational in order to establish communities that are essentially moral.

Appendix C presents a summary of 'The Shepherd Metaphor'. This is a metaphor for leadership that establishes sustainable and moral communities among people in families, local groups and organisations. Indeed, the Leadership Attributes evolved through the early work on this metaphor and subsequent research study.

Appendix D presents the full version of a most unique and poignant verse by Oriah Mountain Dreamer.

Introduction

Appendix E presents Benjamin Franklin's 13 Virtues, which he used as a means of daily reflection.

The Leadership Attributes have evolved into a number of new and different ways of learning for people of all ages. The following products are available through my website: www.vickymcgahey.com:

1. The Leadership Attributes Journal: intended as a companion to this book, this free journal has been created for you to use as you reflect upon the attributes and the questions raised within this book.
2. The Leadership Attributes Game: focusing on the 15 key attributes, the game engages participants in a pursuit that acknowledges their potential to help humankind. The process and subsequent reflection upon the cards encourages rich dialogue that encourages participants to be listening learners.
3. The Leadership Attributes Cards of Reflection: designed to provide additional reflection upon the meaning of each of the 15 attributes, these cards can be used as a daily/weekly reflective practice tool for use by individuals or groups.
4. Young Adult series of books: *The Kingdom of Wizards*.

I wish you well as you journey through the pages of this book on leadership. Take your time – give yourself the gift of time. If you need to do a quick read of it, do so … but do come back and spend some reflective time.

Sincerely,
Vicky McGahey

The lessons learnt on the journey
are more important
than the final destination.
For the lessons will determine
the right destination.

~Vicky McGahey~

Part 1

Chapter 1

Leaders are Born or Leaders are Made?

Since humankind began to come together to form community, this question on the concept of leadership has been debated in many forums. It presents the yin and yang, the black and white, the hot and the cold nature of leadership. Leadership is a double-edged sword and offers two different sides of the coin. The argument given in this book supports a positive and resounding 'yes' to both possibilities.

Leaders are born
and
Leaders are made

Leaders are born, because each and every one of us is born with innate attributes that can be revealed by our actions through the goodness of spirit. These attributes are called Leadership Attributes.

Leaders are made, because each and every one of us can develop these attributes within ourselves to release our leadership potential. It begins through the discovery of our own vision and mission. Then, it is lived through our actions. It is through our actions that relationships are formed, which, in turn, build community.

At some point in time, every one of us will be called to lead. This can be in the smallest of situations or events of life. It is as simple as when someone asks us for advice or when we see a need that requires action. First and foremost, leadership is service.

The following is an adapted story taken from *The Little Brown Book* by Sue and Leo Kane.[1] This book brings the essence of St Mary MacKillop to life through the stories of courage, compassion and kindness that made Mary a formidable and much-loved leader.

Mary MacKillop and the Pub

St Mary MacKillop (St Mary of the Cross) is Australia's first and only saint (canonised on 17 October 2010). Mary is as close to a contemporary saint as one is likely to find. Along with Father Julian Tenison Woods, she founded the Institute of the Sisters of St Joseph at the tender age of 24. The Sisters have worked with the very poor and underprivileged people of the new and growing colonies of Australia and New Zealand since the late 1800s until this present time.

One place the Sisters had founded a school was Port Augusta in South Australia. Unfortunately, a kerosene lamp had exploded in the face of one of the Sisters. As she lay dying, she pleaded to see Mary, who responded quickly and managed to get as far as the town of Mt Remarkable.

Like many country towns, Mt Remarkable had a local pub. It was the afternoon and the pub was full of tired and thirsty farmers looking forward to enjoying a beer and a lively conversation about the days' harvesting of wheat. Mary entered the pub dressed in her habit. One can only imagine, as the figure of a nun entered the bar, the conversation would have quickly turned to silence.

Apparently, Mary turned to the men and said, 'Gentleman! One of my sisters in Port Augusta is dying, and is constantly asking for me. If one of you will lend me a horse, I will ride there.'

In a short period of time, the men had managed to get a pair of horses and a buggy. Three of them drove Mary to the convent as the afternoon sun set. Fortunately, Mary arrived in time to console the Sister. She died knowing that Mary was with her in person and in prayer.

Some argue that leadership does not exist as a formal subject and therefore is not worthy of formal study. However, we cannot ignore the obvious. When people (and animals for that matter) come together, they create hierarchical relationships where one or more individuals are the leader or leaders of a community.

Leadership is a subject that borrows its content from many diverse fields of study and human endeavour – politics, religion, sociology, economics, the military and so on. We cannot ignore the impact of leadership and its influence in the formation of human relationships, the establishment of communities and subsequent actions.

History is splattered with examples of individuals or groups of individuals who led for a whole range of reasons, though it is important to mention that groups of people or a collective have never really brought about change. It has always been an individual within a collective who has led and inspired them into action.

There are any number of ways and different reasons why one becomes a leader. Here are four examples:
- higher ideal
- domination
- chosen
- born.

There are those who seek leadership for some higher ideal and purpose. They often take a personal role in providing direction for their people. Examples would include political and religious leaders, such as George Washington, Pope Francis, St Joan of Arc, Eleanor Roosevelt, Mahatma Gandhi, Abraham Lincoln and Martin Luther King, Jr. Many wealthy, gifted and talented people will often assume a leadership role. Examples include Angelina Jolie, Princess Diana, Sir Bob Geldof, Bill and Melissa Gates and Jamie Oliver, to name a few.

Then, there have always been those who dominate and seek to control people either for their own personal gain or a fanatical belief. They are usually experts in communication and in convincing others that they are right. Classic examples include Adolf Hitler, Benito Mussolini, Osama bin Laden and Saddam Hussein. History is also littered with dictators who forced people to follow them – often kicking and screaming – such as Pol Pot and Idi Amin. In the fullness of time, a dictator's selfish reign usually ends in ruins. Sadly, more often than not, a nation continues to suffer years after the fall of its dictator.

There have also been those who have not sought leadership per se, but their vision and actions have landed them right in the world spotlight. Their very being and natural persona encourages others to listen and follow them. Examples would be Mahatma Gandhi, Mother Teresa of Calcutta, St Mary MacKillop, Eleanor Roosevelt and, more recently, Malala Yousafzai, a teenager shot for campaigning for the rights of women in Pakistan to have an education. And, let's not forget all those who work tirelessly at NGOs (non-government organisations) all over the world.

There are those who are born to lead through their birthright. In modern day reality, these people find themselves more as a figurehead or symbol, rather than a leader with any great power or persuasion. Examples include the remaining royal families, like those of England, Norway and Thailand, or past and present dynasty families, like the Roosevelts and Kennedys. However, through the course of history, individuals from these families have held significant leadership roles and have led by example.

One thing that good (moral) leaders have in common is that the 'essence' of their leadership comes from deep within themselves. For many, they say it is a 'calling' or a yearning to 'become'. Their willingness and ability to listen intuitively to their inner voice is mirrored through their actions, which reflect their beliefs and values.

The rest of this chapter is divided up into sections that will attempt to address the following:

- Why is this book on leadership attributes so important?
- Sensing the urgency for leadership in disruptive times.
- What is the benefit of the book's message – why should I care?
- Women in leadership – how to promote?
- What's wrong with the topic of leadership?
- What is leadership like and what is it about?
- What's in it for me?
- How is this book different ... unique?
- So what should you do now?

Why is this book on leadership attributes so important?

World leaders are struggling to cope with the fast-changing environment of world politics, which brings with it crises in housing and finance, nations in civil war and, therefore, more refugees and migrants to countries already struggling to remain economically viable.[2]

The onslaught of this globalisation has been instrumental in bringing about the need for people to develop tolerance, the ability to see diversity as a strength and, at the very least, to accept change. Such willingness to listen and value the human rights of others is the essence of forming moral and good communities.[3] Moral communities engage in the sharing of principles, values and beliefs in open and honest dialogue with all members of a community.[4] Leaders play a key role in this dialogue by ensuring that all voices are heard. These communities exist in organisations, community groups and wherever people come together.

The rapid and destructive rise in terrorism and wars based on religious and cultural intolerance is not good for humankind nor should it be tolerated and accepted complacently. All too often we see atrocities occurring under the misguided claim of religious and/or political freedom, the misery and suffering of those in war-torn countries and refugee camps and the plight of illegal immigrants who take extreme measures to escape tyranny and war. The future of humankind will be determined by the small acts of mercy, kindness and tolerance each one of us shows to each other. Eleanor Roosevelt stated in her proclamation of human rights:

> Where, after all, do universal human rights begin? In small places, close to home - so close and so small that they cannot be seen on any maps of the world. Yet they are the world of the individual person; the neighborhood he lives in; the school or college he attends; the factory, farm, or office where he works. Such are the places where every man, woman, and child seeks equal justice, equal opportunity, equal dignity without discrimination.

Unless these rights have meaning there, they have little meaning anywhere. Without concerted citizen action to uphold them close to home, we shall look in vain for progress in the larger world.[5]

Humankind is seeking purpose – it always has been. To see so many people around the world come together to build shrines and grieve for those who have lost their lives in senseless acts of terrorism is reassuring, comforting and good. But these are often one-off events. The same sentiment needs to be felt as we engage with each other on a daily basis; the same sentiment that evokes empathy, compassion, tolerance and respect. It is a sentiment built upon faith, hope and charity (love).

As previously stated, the underlying premise of this book is that leadership can be developed within each and every one of us. Leadership begins within the individual as they make a stand for what they believe, either through word or deed. This is important because we need to provide a future not just for ourselves and our family and friends but for the whole of humankind. We all need to become part of the global movement towards goodness, forgiveness and reconciliation.

Now, more than ever, we require leadership at every level of human existence. However, we must remain realistic in our expectations of leaders. We fool ourselves when we expect our leaders to behave better than we ourselves behave, and it is quite hypocritical to do so. Leaders are first and foremost human.

Not all of us seek leadership roles in work and community life, yet we are often called upon to display the attributes that we expect our leaders to display. We do this in order to form good relationships, which, in turn, establish good and sustainable communities.

As mentioned in the Introduction, there is a shameful lack of women in leadership roles throughout the world – in business organisations, NGOs, local community and, often, in family life. This gender imbalance is in need of an immediate response if we are truly to become the best humankind can be – a shared partnership built upon the foundation stones of tolerance, authenticity and respect. And, without doubt, these need to be created in a atmosphere of love for humanity and the blessings of humanity – all this regardless of religion, race or creed.

The leadership attributes described in this book are not just a set of ideals to try to live up to when seeking leadership or working in leadership roles. They are little gems that you can bring forth every moment of every day to make this world a more beautiful place for yourself and others. They can also be a 'game changer'. The use of the attributes can cause a shift in your own sense of self-being and purpose. However, it is hoped that as you grow through the use of the attributes you will be blessed and graced with seeing the joy of humanity. In this way, as so many great leaders have shown, you can live your life to the full and be happy while making a difference.

Sensing the urgency for leadership in disruptive times

There has always been human suffering through wars, terrorism, floods, fires and drought. However, the wonders of modern communication and social media mean we can see events as they are unfolding from any place in the world and at any time of the day or night. It is in our living rooms 24/7. With our media devices, we can access such information at any time. The modern world of virtual teams, telecommunication and cyberspace can lead to continuous disruption within the workplace, community and home.

This is not all bad. However, leaders need to remain vigilant for changes in the marketplace that can have a dramatic effect on their organisation. These changes are aptly termed 'disruptive'.[6]

The days seem to be shorter and we seem driven to do more in the space of a day. We know more, can find more and can do more. There is a sense of urgency within us to get to somewhere. Still, several questions remain:

- Where are we going?
- Who is leading us? Or are we leading ourselves? Towards what?
- Are the world leaders to be trusted?

There is a need for a sense of purpose within this world and, sadly, it is not easily found. It is why world leaders struggle to get their message of peace across. There are two likely reasons for this inability. At times, the behaviour of some of the world leaders leaves much to be desired and people lose trust and faith in their leaders. To lose trust and faith in a person is something that can never be fully repaired. You will learn more about that in the Leadership Attributes of Trust and Trustworthy. The second is more personal. It strikes at the heart and soul of your being … who am I, why I am here, and what direction should I take?

In a world that seems, at times, to be spinning out of control, we need to search deep within ourselves for the attributes that will help to lead us in the right direction. Then, as individuals, we need to come together as a collective to guide and nurture each other towards establishing communities where all voices are heard.

It is imperative that we, as individuals, be the leaders in community who sense the urgent need to guide each other towards a direction that is good and true. And, while moving towards our destination, we should ensure that the means we employ to get to that destination are also good and true. We must always ensure the moral imperative 'to do no harm' prevails in what we think, say and do as a person.

The steps we take towards our goal are a journey. Never allow the destination to become more important than the journey. The journey is where the lessons of life are learnt and those experiences are what make life unique, precious and good.

There is also the need for creativity and innovation in organisations, community groups and family life in order to keep the dialogue – whatever that may be – alive. This raises serious questions:

- What inspires us to follow some people and not others?
- What is it?
- What is the secret?

There is no secret. 'Why' we follow basically comes down to three simple reasons:

- The person (attributes).
- The message they are telling (selling).
- The 'buy into' – what's in it for me/us (support).

The research, as cited in this book, essentially sought to find out 'why' people follow others. It revealed that it is the person themself – what lies within the person; in other words, the attributes of the person. These attributes are the inherent qualities that encourage certain behaviour or actions from a person.

The second reason is the 'message'. However, the message can be masked or not listened to if there is no trust, faith or confidence in the person selling it. The 'buy into' aspect can also be overlooked if there is no or little credibility held for the person who is presenting the message.

As previously mentioned, the study revealed 15 attributes that a person needs to develop within themselves when striving to build a community within an organisation, community group or family. Part 2 of this book describes each of the attributes in detail (see also Appendix A). Out of the 15 attributes, six were found to be the most significant when trying to build a community.

People have asked how they can develop these attributes within themselves. It is through reflection upon our experiences of life both in thought, word and deed. This enables us to see and develop these attributes within ourselves. The attributes are described in each section, but the reader is asked to reflect upon several questions as they read the stories, research findings and ponder their own development and plan of action.

What is the benefit of the book's message – why should I care?

The material in this book has been chosen to excite you and to lift your spirits to help you look beyond. It is given in the hope that you'll realise:

- leaders are born and leaders are made;
- leadership attributes exist within each and every one of us.

As previously stated, leadership is a concept and construct borne out of personal perceptions and beliefs. In this sense, it can be described as an unseen natural phenomenon.

The work of this book is offered as a means to build up strength within those who are on their way towards a leadership role, but equally, it offers insights that will benefit all readers, not just those seeking leadership. Those who are finding it difficult to find their place in this world and those who find the landscape of their reality often difficult to traverse will find the book immensely useful too.

We must strive to be the best we can possibly be and allow our souls to grow in ways and in depths that reach beyond what we dream we can do. In doing so, we release the potential within and can perform deeds far greater than we expect of ourselves. This potential is possible regardless of race or creed, religious beliefs or political persuasion, our work or educational status, lifestyle or economic situation.

The following verse, *The Invitation* by Oriah Mountain Dreamer, strikes right at the heart of the matter. This is only a small part of an inspiring poem (see Appendix D for full version).

The Invitation

It doesn't interest me
what you do for a living.
I want to know
what you ache for
and if you dare to dream
of meeting your heart's longing ...

I want to know
if you can sit with pain
mine or your own
without moving to hide it
or fade it
or fix it. ...

It doesn't interest me
who you know
or how you came to be here.
I want to know if you will stand
in the centre of the fire
with me
and not shrink back.

> It doesn't interest me
> where or what or with whom
> you have studied.
> I want to know
> what sustains you
> from the inside
> when all else falls away.
>
> I want to know
> if you can be alone
> with yourself
> and if you truly like
> the company you keep
> in the empty moments.[7]

The content of this book reaches beyond political correctness and it cannot be shaped by old paradigms. It thrives on fresh insight and on self-integrity. It seeks the truth that lies within. That truth is called 'the knowing'. In other words, what you feel and know.

So, whether you possess a simple heart or you have ambitions of being a great leader or just a better person, whether you're trying to make it to the top or just make it through till tomorrow, hopefully this book will inspire you to 'become'.

The benefit of reading such a book is in the time you give to reflection. As you read, reflect upon the leadership attributes, the questions, the research findings and the stories. Then, begin to recall stories of your own. You should start to question and find ways to put each attribute into action within your daily life.

Hopefully, you will begin to notice changes in your life. In this way, you will become a leader and not just a leader of yourself, but of others as well – for people will see this within you. They'll see it through your words and actions.

> There is no ending without a beginning.
> Beginning and ending go hand in hand
> to form a continuous cycle.
> ~Vicky McGahey~

Women in leadership – how to promote?

At this point, I think it fair and just to comment about an issue close to my heart – the lack of women in leadership roles in most facets of life.

Leaders are born
and
Leaders are made

I would add to this profound statement that this is true of either gender. In other words: leaders are born and leaders are made, regardless of gender.

A 2013 report, based on 600 participants, found 93.2% believe there are barriers to gender equality in the workplace (CEDA, 2013).[8] Gender discrimination still exists in organisations, as it has done for decades. And, gender discrimination remains in community groups and sometimes in the harsh reality of family life. Sadly, such discrimination is often supported by women themselves. The reason for this deserves investigation, along with the statements we continuously hear, like 'a woman's place is in the home.' These serve only as a put-down and have no place in a rational argument or debate on gender equality.

There is a world crisis in gender inequality. Many argue that the leader should be chosen on merit – and rightly so! But, there is a gross and often deliberate neglect to mentor, coach and help women to develop the skills and expertise so that they too can be considered for a leadership role. And those women and men who think it is 'just business'! Shame! You do yourself, family and humanity a gross disservice – one that, when exposed, may bring your leadership aspirations to an end.

What's wrong with the topic of leadership?

The problem with this topic is that everyone is an expert on the subject. We learn about leaders and leadership from a very young age – for example, from our parents and the family members who guide us. Then, we see leadership through extended community and the role models we meet.

As we grow older, we begin to realise that leadership is more than just the roles we play or the job that we have. We learn that leadership also has its shortcomings. It's a risky business being a leader. You are open to criticism along with being held responsible and accountable for not only your own actions but also for the actions of others who serve with you. Yet essentially, we know that someone needs to stand up and just get on with it.

Then, there is that word 'power'. So often we see leadership as just a power play. Yes, it can be that. At times, that is exactly what it is for those who seek to control. They are not interested in leading in the service of others, only in serving their own self-interests. However, they will inevitably lose that power and their leadership. History has proven this time and time again. Dictatorship, whether by an individual or individuals, will come to an end. Sadly, more often than not, the end is a disaster not only for themself/themselves but for those they led.

From a global perspective, the current leadership qualities demonstrated by many world leaders have been found to be limited and, at times, non-existent. Far too many individuals accept positions of leadership and then allow political undercurrents to dominate and erode their vision, mission and the action needed to form relationships that build sustainable communities (nations). Why seek the job in the first place? The only plausible answer is 'to satisfy their ego'.

Seriously, if you seek to be a leader, then, as an individual, you must believe that the attributes that can foster relationships and build sustainable communities lie within you – believe that you can lead and make the world around you a better place.

Then, we must stop letting the end justify the means. As previously stated, the journey is where the lessons of life are learnt. It is those experiences that make life unique, precious and good.

What is leadership like and what is it about?

Leadership is a concept or construct found in the perception of others. The fact that others perceive there is leadership, see that there is a leader and are prepared to be followers is proof it exists. Leadership exists within the constructs of human spirit, thought, word and action.

However, leadership is not a solo sport! Franklin D. Roosevelt once said, 'It's a terrible thing to look over your shoulder when you are trying to lead – and to find no-one there.'

You're not a leader without followers.[9] Leadership is about persuasion. Leadership is a human capacity and ability to persuade others to follow you. Leadership within followership; followership through leadership. Leadership and followership require the gathering of people. In business, this is called team building. From the wider perspective of humankind, it is called community building.

But how do you do this? As previously mentioned, there are reasons why people follow: the person themself (attributes), the message they are telling (selling) and the 'why buy into' – what's in it for me and/or us (support). But, it is the person that is the most significant reason – the person's attributes and their willingness to display these attributes through their words and actions.

Essentially, leadership by a good leader will consist of several 'awarenesses'. These have a religious/spiritual connotation about them, but do not be put off by this – they are so much more. To be aware is to:

1. Be in tune with yourself – *Sensing the spirit within*. Such sensing includes knowing your principles, values and beliefs. What do you feel?
2. Be in tune with the environment around you – *Sensing the spirit without*. This sensing includes asking several questions, like: What is going on around you at a personal level and at a professional level?
3. Be in grace – *A graceful vision of a grace-filled mission is a call to action*. Grace is a state of being and is a spiritual presence. Grace can be an ideal that we strive to reach.

4. Be willing to serve – *Leadership is service.* Sometimes the service involves the willingness to share the role.
5. Be willing to step down – *Preparing others for the role and planning your exit point.* This is known as succession planning. It involves knowing when to step down and determining who/what will replace you. Then do it in style and with grace.

The potential to be a leader exists within all of us. As the premise and content of this book presents, good leadership is built upon the foundation stones of the leadership attributes. These attributes are within us and lived through our words and actions. Each of us needs the opportunity to discover them within ourselves and then to rise to the occasion.

What's in it for me?

At different times of our lives we are called upon to be leaders and to show the attributes discussed in this book. By reading, reflecting upon the questions raised and the stories told, you will achieve the following:

1. Personal satisfaction through a better understanding of yourself. This includes a realisation that you are capable of leading (whenever called upon to do so and in any forum).
2. You will appreciate that others have the potential to lead.
3. Know when to step up and use your gifts and talents in the service of others. This includes knowing when to step aside and allow others to lead.
4. Be able to form leadership teams where everyone has a leadership role to play. Leadership is a shared experience.
5. Know that leadership is more than just a power play. Leadership is about being authentic, transparent and accountable in your use of power and in the relationships you build with others.
6. Use the three-stage process of leadership actions – gathering, pathfinding and presence (always there). These are discussed in Chapter 10.

In preparation for when you will be asked to step up, this book will be of great value.

Summation thus far

There is an obvious need for improved leadership within our world. Thus far I have argued that we all have the ability to lead. We can use our inborn attributes (Leadership Attributes) to persuade others to listen and to follow us.

To bring it together, here are some general statements:

1. Leaders are born and leaders are made, regardless of gender.
2. Leadership is a call to service.
3. Leadership is first and foremost a journey within. To be a good and wise leader begins and ends within.
4. Leadership is making use of the innate human attributes within us (Leadership Attributes). These can be used to influence others to listen and follow us. Each and every one of us has these leadership attributes.
5. Leadership is not a solo sport.
6. Leadership within followership; followership through leadership.
7. Leadership involves establishing relationships that, in turn, establish community.
8. Leadership is persuasion.
9. Leadership is the transparent and authentic use of power.
10. Never allow the destination to become more important than the journey. The journey is where the lessons of life are learnt and those lessons are what make life unique, precious and good. So, be thankful and gracious in accepting the experiences and lessons of life.

Leadership viewed in this way will build a community that is essentially moral (good) and based upon principles, values and beliefs where life is cherished as the precious gift.

How is this book different ... unique?

Many books on leadership describe leadership as a list of things you can do to make it happen.

As previously stated, it is a concept, a construct, an idea that is founded through the perceptions of others. The most important perception is that of the individual and the belief that we ourselves can be better than we believe ourselves capable of being. In this way, we begin to build worthwhile relationships and, therefore, community where we are never alone.

The Leadership Attributes as described within this book will enable you to influence others to listen and follow you as you strive to build community in the home, organisation and wider community.

At times we need to rise to the occasion and to take the lead, at least for a while. Hopefully, this book will help you discern when it is time for you to lead or to step back. For, as a shepherd – as the leader of his flock – would practise:

> There are times when the shepherd will be out in front guiding the sheep, and there are times when the shepherd will walk behind pushing and prodding the sheep along. But mostly, the shepherd will walk alongside the sheep and within the flock. (McGahey, 2003)[10]

Being able to discern when it is the right time to be out in front or at the back or walking alongside is the 'essence of leadership'. The idea of leading like a shepherd is discussed throughout the book and is more fully described in Appendix C.

By working through the questions, the stories given, and developing your own stories, as well as the time you give to reflection, you will begin to see these attributes within yourself and within others. Then you will begin to sense the 'essence of leadership' – when to walk in front or behind or walk alongside.

So what should you do now?

Read the book, reflect, discern and start to ask yourself the questions within each section. Begin to form your own questions and recall your own stories. Begin to believe in yourself as both a leader and a follower. It is through following that we lead.

> Leadership within followership;
> followership through leadership.

The next chapter was not originally intended and is an addition after the first rough draft of the book. However, it is the missing piece that brings purpose and direction to the rest of the book. It details the journey towards realising your potential to lead and the attributes that lie within.

Chapter 2

'Becoming'

> I believe that science has great beauty.
> A scientist in his laboratory is not a mere technician;
> he is also a child confronting natural phenomena that
> impress him as though they were fairy tales.
>
> **Marie Curie**

Before launching into the attributes, I believe it is best to step back and give you time to reflect upon what you already know about yourself and your journey. Hopefully, this will reveal just a little of what might be as you 'become'.

To 'become'! What does it mean? The parable below may help to sharpen your thoughts. This story is a modified version.[1]

The Parable of the Pencil

A long, long time ago there lived a pencil maker. He made a range of different coloured pencils. He loved the work and was renowned throughout the land as being the best of the pencil makers.

One day, he crafted a very special pencil. Just before he was about to put the pencil into its box, he thought he should offer some advice to his new creation. He held the pencil gently and spoke: 'There are a few things you need to know! Number one: you will be able to do many great things, but only if you allow yourself to be held in someone's hand like I am holding you now,' he said, as he turned his creation slowly.

'The second thing is, unfortunately,' said the pencil maker hesitantly, 'you will experience a painful sharpening from time to time, but you'll need it to become the best pencil you can possibly be.'

Smiling at the pencil, he continued, 'Number three: fortunately, you will be able to correct any mistakes you make,' as he pointed to the eraser at the top of her head.

He paused for a moment and then said, 'Fourthly, the most important part of you will always be what's inside of you.'

The pencil maker placed the pencil in its box. He gazed upon this little masterpiece and said, 'Fifth and finally, on every surface you are used on you must always leave your mark. No matter what the condition. You must continue to write.'

The pencil looked up from its case into the eyes of its creator. It understood, and promised to remember what it had just been told. The pencil promised that it would live with purpose always in its heart.

Put yourself in the place of the pencil and you'll see that this story is the 'reality of life'. We need to be held and, at times, given a gentle prod to lift our game and to sharpen up. There are times when we have to admit our mistakes, take the flack and do our best to rectify them. And, with that knowledge, know that redemption and forgiveness are always close at hand.

Just as the essence of the pencil comes from its core, we often forget that it is what lies within us that is the most important. In other words, who we are and who we are becoming.

As the pencil maker said: 'you must always leave your mark.' We should do the same no matter what the condition or situation we find ourselves in.

This, however, does raise a few questions: What sort of mark do we want to leave? What about the colour of the pencil? What colour would inspire you?

I believe we have but one life in this part of heaven. The next life remains unknown. I believe the only sure thing is that what you do in this life will impact on the next life. So, choose the colour wisely and sharpen the pencil. Make your mark and make it a good one.

Always draw upon your self-knowledge with integrity, authenticity and transparency.

There are countless stories to be told about 'becoming' – which we hear as we grow up and as we continue to 'grow up' through adulthood. Experiencing that 'Ah! Now I get it!' moment. These are told by storytellers, found in books, and shared in movies and other media. Some of these are shared with you in this book.

Many of the stories are about average people who rose to do extraordinary things. There are stories about famous innovative people – some of whom were leaders, and some of whom were atheists or agnostic or at least spent part of their lives believing so. There are fairy tales, fables and parables. Some are old, others are modern, but all relate to the teaching in this book – the development of attributes that lie within. These attributes are essential for us to become a unique person who has the potential to lead. The following story speaks to the heart and is from the movie: *The Smurfs*.[2]

It Comes from the Heart – The Smurfs

In a cleverly animated children's movie called *The Smurfs*, Papa Smurf is speaking with a human called Patrick, whose wife is about to have a baby. Patrick is nervous about becoming a father for the first time and whether or not he will be a good father. (In case you do not know what Smurfs are – they are tiny blue creatures that live in a parallel world to ours. By misfortune, they end up in our world and are being chased by a villainous wizard called Gargamel and his crazy cat Azrael.)

Patrick and his wife Grace are helping the Smurfs to return home. Papa Smurf and Patrick shared a quiet moment on the roof of an apartment block.

'Doesn't it freak you out sometimes? Having all those little guys dependent on you. I mean what if you screw up? How did you know that you were ready?' asked Patrick of Papa Smurf.

'Let me ask you something,' replied Papa Smurf. 'Why did you come for us today when your Grace called?'

'She needed me,' replied Patrick, 'I could hear it in her voice.'

'Hmm ... Hmm! Well! That is what being a Papa is! When it comes time you just do,' smiled Papa Smurf. 'And knowing what to do does not come from up here - in your head. It comes from here - your heart.'

'You are a good Papa, Papa!' smiled Patrick.

'And you will be a good Papa too,' replied Papa Smurf.

How true are those words: 'Knowing what to do does not come from your head. It comes from your heart.'

Patrick was learning how to cope with his fear of fatherhood in much the same way as coping with any fear. One should always seek the answers from deep within. For what is felt is more important than what is thought.

Taking this point a step further, the answers to life's big questions lie within us and not without. The environment and people around us are there to help awaken within us that which we already know. I call this 'the knowing'. Some call it the conscience. A more religious person may call it the Holy Spirit.

Remember what the pencil maker said to the pencil: 'the most important part of you will always be what's inside of you.' This represents the inward journey towards 'becoming'.

HRH Queen Elizabeth II is one world leader who has asked people to search deep within themselves to find their inner goodness. In her Diamond Jubilee speech to Parliament during 2012, she spoke of the need for people to grow in resilience, tolerance and ingenuity.[3]

While visiting Australia, Mary Robinson, past President of Ireland and United Nations ambassador, spoke about world poverty. She cited the United Nations as stressing the need for people and corporations to develop integrity, transparency and accountability in all they do.[4]

Warren Bennis was a leadership theory pioneer and guru. During an interview in 2010, Bennis said he was not religious, but that his next book – which he never did write – would be on the importance of grace. It would include discussion around the concepts of 'generosity, respect, redemption and sacrifices. All of which sound vaguely spiritual, but all of which I think are going to be required for leadership.'[5]

Bennis hinted at the spiritual nature of leadership. This is a concept not uncommon in recent literature and many courses on the subject. The spirit is not confined to religious or spiritual thought. The Christian faith and other religious faiths teach of the sacrificial and redemptive nature of human life and how the Holy Spirit is forever present to guide humankind back to God.

The qualities or ideals of generosity, respect, resilience, tolerance, ingenuity, integrity, transparency, accountability (responsibility), with the addition of authenticity, can be fostered in practices through the attributes and actions of a leader as described within this book.[6] In this way, grace-filled and authentic relationships are built and nurtured. Several writers in the field of leadership have realised the significance of relationships (personal and group) in organisations and the formation of communities.[7]

But how do you do this? How do you form communities? The answer lies within – you develop the qualities/virtues or what this book terms 'attributes within yourself'. So, how do you find and develop these attributes within yourself? One well-known figurehead and leader developed a technique, as shown in the following story (see also Appendix E).[8]

The 13 Virtues of Benjamin Franklin

Even though he was already well on the road to becoming an iconic historical figure, when he was in his mid-20s, Benjamin Franklin resolved that he would improve his life. Franklin did this by developing an examen (the contemplation of your own thoughts, desires and conduct). In this examen, he developed 13 virtues consisting of temperance, silence, order, resolution, frugality, industry, sincerity, justice, moderation, cleanliness, tranquillity, chastity and humility.

Franklin was a practical person, so he ensured that each virtue could be described through action. For example, silence was defined as 'speak not but what may benefit others or yourself; avoid trifling conversation.' This implied avoiding gossip, negative talk and any idle chatter.

Every week, Franklin focused on one of these virtues. In the morning, he would contemplate how he was going to use this virtue in the service of others. Then, in the evening, he would sit down and recount his day to see if he had actually done as he had planned.

Franklin kept this up for many years and, in his late 70s, he attributed his success in life to this practice. He found that it had helped him to recognise both his strengths and his limitations. Franklin realised he had a very strong personality and that he needed to overcome his pride. However, he was sensible enough to realise that he could never rid himself of all pride (as having some is a healthy thing) – he just had to keep it in check. He felt that perfection would never be achieved. Franklin believed he had led a better and happier life than would have been the case without his daily examen.

By staying in touch with his virtues and turning them into achievable goals that he valued, Franklin could 'become' the best he could possibly be – for himself and for others. Through his daily ritual, Franklin tuned into his intuition and was able to recognise opportunities as they arose.

There is a Hindu parable about being aware of opportunities even if you are not really ready for them. A greater part of 'becoming' is awareness of self before an awareness of others. From this awareness, opportunities will arise. This version of the parable is an adaptation from *Kitchen Table Wisdom* by Rachel Naomi Remen.[9]

The Bag of Gold – Shiva and Shakti

Shiva, the divine god, married Shakti, a goddess. They caringly watch over the world and in particular the lives of humankind. They witness human frailty and suffering, as well as the joy and beauty of human life.

One day, Shakti observed a poor old man walking down a well-worn path. He was muttering to himself and seemed tired and not very happy. 'Oh! Woe is me! I have no opportunity and no hope.'

His clothing was torn and his sandals were tied up with twine. Shakti was moved with compassion and searched within the soul of the old man to see if he was good and true of spirit.

She turned to her husband Shiva and asked him to give the old man some gold.

Shiva, who had also been observing the old man replied, 'I cannot grant your request, dear wife.'

Shakti was quite surprised at this reply. 'But why not, beloved? You are god of the universe. Surely you can do this simple kindness?'

'Yes! I could! But he is not yet ready to receive it.'

Shakti became quite upset. 'Surely,' she pleaded, 'you could drop one small bag of gold at his feet.'

Shiva does not wish to see his wife sad, so he finally agreed, and dropped a bag of gold along the path.

The old man was still muttering to himself. 'I wonder if I will find food and shelter tonight or will I go hungry again? It is starting to get late! Oh! Woe is me!'

As he walked around the bend, he noticed what looked like a rock on the pathway. 'Oh! Thank goodness I was looking down and noticed that rock,' he muttered, 'I could have tripped on it and, at the very worst, ruined these tattered sandals of mine even further.'

The old man very carefully stepped around the rock and went on his way. The rock was, in fact, the bag of gold. He was totally oblivious to the missed opportunity and riches to be had.

Life does drop bags of gold as we navigate through our human journey. We just need to be aware and open to possibilities – to see these moments as opportunities to grow, to gather riches and richness in life. Too often we let our worries and fears disguise the bags of gold – as the old man did – regarding them as yet another nuisance, another hurdle to jump or mountain to climb. We beat ourselves up, never realising that we are all blessed with bags of gold. We just need to see that our 'problems are only solutions waiting to be found' (Anon.). Our problems are solved by tackling them head-on and not by walking around them.

From a leadership perspective, it is hoped that upon discovering the gold, we would spend it in the service of others and not just on ourselves.

'Becoming'

Perhaps the bags of gold are bags of grace, where each piece of gold is a virtue, quality or an attribute. Therefore, become aware of your own virtues and attributes, using these to awaken the power of your intuition. Then, through reflection upon your actions you can 'become'. In this way, you can find the courage to follow your heart and transform your life.

Yet another story about uncovering or revealing the golden treasure hidden within each of us is the story of the Golden Buddha statue. This true story is an adaptation based on the original version in *Chicken Soup for the Soul* by Jack Canfield and Mark Victor Hansen.[10]

The Golden Buddha

In 1957, a group of monks had to relocate a clay Buddha from their monastery to a new location. The monastery was to be relocated to make room for the development of a highway through Bangkok. Measuring approximately 4 metres from base to top and 3 metres across the lap from knee to knee, and weighing 5.5 tonnes, the statue was made several hundred years ago.

When the crane began to lift the giant idol, the weight of it was so tremendous that it began to crack. So, they placed the statue on the ground. Soon, the afternoon rain began to fall and so they placed a large canvas tarp over the statue to protect it.

Later that evening, the head monk went to check on the Buddha. He shone his flashlight under the tarp to see if the statue was dry. He noticed the crack and a large chunk broken off and lying on the floor. As he took a closer look at the crack, he saw a glimmer of light. He wondered if there might be something underneath the clay. After fetching a chisel and hammer from the monastery, he began to chip away at the clay. Many hours of labour went by before the monk stood face-to-face with the extraordinary, solid gold Buddha.

It is believed that the 'plastering over' took place before the destruction of the Ayutthaya Kingdom by Burmese invaders in 1767. Unfortunately, it appears that the Burmese slaughtered all the Siamese monks, so the Golden Buddha – estimated to be worth US$250 million –

remained hidden from view until the 1950s. The temple that houses the Golden Buddha was rebuilt in 2010.

We often cover up our true selves for numerous reasons. 'Becoming' can be a bit like peeling an onion – one layer at a time until the true nature of ourselves is revealed. To be a good leader you need to peel back the layers to discover and reveal your attributes to yourself first. Then, through your actions you reveal the 'golden' attributes to others.

There are many writers in the field, like Bolman and Deal (2011), Bowling (2011), Starratt (1996) and others, who believe that to become a good leader (the best you can be) requires a venture into one's soul.[11] This includes taking the time to stop and listen to the still-small voice within.[12] For many, listening to the small voice is essentially a spiritual experience and can be a blending of spirit and truth.[13] Though many would claim there is no empirical evidence for the existence of a soul, it is still a concept a little difficult to dismiss when a survey by the Barna Group in 2003 revealed that eight out of ten people in America believe in a human soul and an afterlife.[14]

This venture into one's soul is a discovery of self and the giving of gifts, such as the gifts of love, the gifts of authorship (freeing the intelligence) and the gifts of significance (celebration of rituals, stories and ceremonies). The journey is not without risk. It will take courage to accept our imperfections and to be vulnerable.[15] This is just as the parable of the pencil demonstrated (see page 36).

As continuously stated, you're not a leader without followers and, therefore, there is a need for the formation of community. So there is much to be gained through authentic, transparent and accountable relationships that reside within community. There is also a need for valuing the heart, soul and mind of other people, as well as developing and nurturing their gifts and talents.[16] In this way you build a strong community whether it is within an organisation, local group or in your own family.

One of the best ways towards 'becoming' is through service. There is a wonderful true story about a nineteenth-century princess who discovered herself through service. Her name was Princess Alice of Battenberg.

A Story of Service – Princess Alice of Battenberg

Princess Alice of Battenberg was the mother of Prince Philip, Duke of Edinburgh, and mother-in-law of Queen Elizabeth II.

Princess Alice was born at Windsor Castle on 25 February 1885, and died at Buckingham Palace on 5 December 1969. She was one of those people who lived her life with great courage, fortitude and conviction. She was blessed with the gifts of goodness, patience, kindness, generosity, faithfulness, joy and charity. However, she was born into this world profoundly deaf. Through the love and drive of her mother, Alice was encouraged to learn to lip-read in three different languages – English, German and French. When she married into Greek royalty, she taught herself Greek.

Princess Alice was determined to live her life in the way of her own choosing. During the Balkan War, Alice served as a nurse and her husband served in the military. During World War I, the family was exiled from Greece.

Sadly, Princess Alice had mental issues, and was committed to a mental institution, suffering from schizophrenia. It is reported that she was even treated by Sigmund Freud. It is said the treatment was brutal and barbaric. Eventually, Alice was released and disappeared from royal and public life for a number of years until 1936, by which time her marriage had ended.

However, Princess Alice eventually returned to Greece in 1938. During World War II, she worked for the Red Cross and helped those in need by organising soup kitchens, nursing of the sick and child-sheltering facilities. Princess Alice would smuggle in medical supplies after visiting her sister Louise, who was married to the Crown Prince of Sweden.

In recent times, it has been revealed that Alice secretly hid a Jewish refugee family, the Cohens, in her home during the occupation of Greece. She took a great risk, considering she was in the public eye, and the Nazis knew that the princess was up to something but they never caught her. It is believed she defied a German officer as they searched her home. She was even interviewed by the Gestapo and used her deafness to pretend she did not understand their questions.

In 1949, Princess Alice founded an Orthodox nursing order of nuns known as the Christian Sisterhood of Martha and Mary. She sold her jewellery to build a convent and orphanage in a poor suburb of Athens.

At the coronation of Queen Elizabeth II in 1952, Princess Alice, the mother in-law to the Queen, proceeded down the aisle as a lone figure in her grey habit. In the pews, she sat as the head of her family.

Sadness and struggle as a member of the Royal family seemed to follow Princess Alice, for in 1967 she was once again exiled after the fall of King Constantine II of Greece. However, she was invited by her son and daughter-in-law to live at Buckingham Palace. Princess Alice died two years later.

In 1988, according to her wishes, the Duke of Edinburgh was allowed to inter her ashes in Jerusalem at the Church of Mary Magdalene on the Mount of Olives. In 1994, she was awarded 'Righteous Among the Nations' at Yad Vashem, and in 2010, she was posthumously named a 'Hero of the Holocaust' by the British Government.

Princess Alice did not allow her disability, her inability to hear, to impact on the way she wished to live. Her strength of character and knowledge of her own gifts and talents and her willingness and ability to use these in the service of others was paramount. Princess Alice was a role model for leadership and a person who displayed the qualities of a saint.

Summary – to 'become'

This chapter has revealed several key features to our journey on 'becoming'. These include, but are not exclusive of:

1. What lies within us is most important.
2. Seek the answer to life's questions from within – what is felt is more important than what is thought.

3. Venture into your soul. Become aware of your attributes (qualities and virtues) and gifts. Reflect upon these daily as Benjamin Franklin did.
4. Lead with grace – be generous, respectful and redemptive and make sacrifices.
5. Become a courageous model of transparency and authenticity. Be accountable.
6. Help others to find themselves and 'become'.
7. Never allow the destination to become more important than the journey. The journey is where the lessons of life are learnt and those lessons are what make life unique, precious and good. So, be thankful and gracious in accepting the experiences and lessons of life.

To 'become' will take courage and a considerable amount of the 'gift of your time'. Congratulations on reading thus far … you have already begun the journey!

The following chapters (Chapters 3–9) on the Leadership Attributes will help in the understanding of the process of 'becoming'. Practical advice and applications are given in subsequent chapters (Chapters 10 and 11 and the appendices).

Part 2

Chapter 3

The Model of the Leadership Attributes

*It is not more light that is needed in the world,
it is more warmth.
We will not die of darkness but of cold.*

Jenny Read[1]

The essence of leadership is poignantly expressed in this quote by sculptor Jenny Read. It is leadership that shines like a beacon to attract people, but also keeps people together through the sheer warmth emanating from the source — the warmth is what will draw people towards the leader. This warmth is a person's qualities or virtues. In this book, they are called Leadership Attributes and they form the major focus of Part 2.

The Leadership Attributes emerged through an eight-year study that included interviewing educational leaders about the most significant attributes for establishing a moral (good) community.[2] Such a community can exist within an organisation, not-for-profit organisations, local groups, and in the family.

A model was devised so that the attributes could be described and presented in a logical form. The Leadership Attributes Model is discussed in the following chapters.

The model consists of 15 attributes. These are displayed in the diagram (see pages 52–53) as separate satellite attributes that orbit around the central point labelled Attributes. There are six key attributes (Integrity, Prophecy, Empathy, Intuition, Judgment and Communication). Each of these key attributes has one or two satellite attributes linked to it.

The Leadership Attributes Model

Chapters 4–9 will present each key attribute and its associated satellite attribute(s):

- Chapter 4   Integrity – satellite attributes of Trust and Trustworthy.
- Chapter 5   Prophecy – satellite attributes of Transcendence and Faith.
- Chapter 6   Empathy – satellite attributes of Compassion and Passion.
- Chapter 7   Intuition – satellite attribute of Risk
- Chapter 8   Judgment – satellite attribute of Diversity
- Chapter 9   Communication – satellite attribute of Consistency

A diagram of the Leadership Attributes Model is shown overleaf.

Each chapter is designed around a similar format. This is to ensure that there is some consistency with the message and the manner in which it is given. This is also for ease of reading and reflection. You should be able to read each chapter as a single entity.

Each chapter begins with a visual of the key attribute and its associated satellite attribute(s). The description includes a quotation, a motto, a symbol and a simple definition. These are given so as to encourage the reader to stop and reflect upon the attribute. The idea is to discover what the attribute means for the reader at this particular moment in time. Then, a series of questions is given for the reader to ponder as they read the stories, the research findings and other information. At the conclusion of each chapter is the attribute in reflective action. This is a step-by-step guide for the reader to reflect upon and put into daily practice.

The Leadership Attributes Journal is free and available as a companion to this book; it can be downloaded from my website: www.vickymcgahey.com

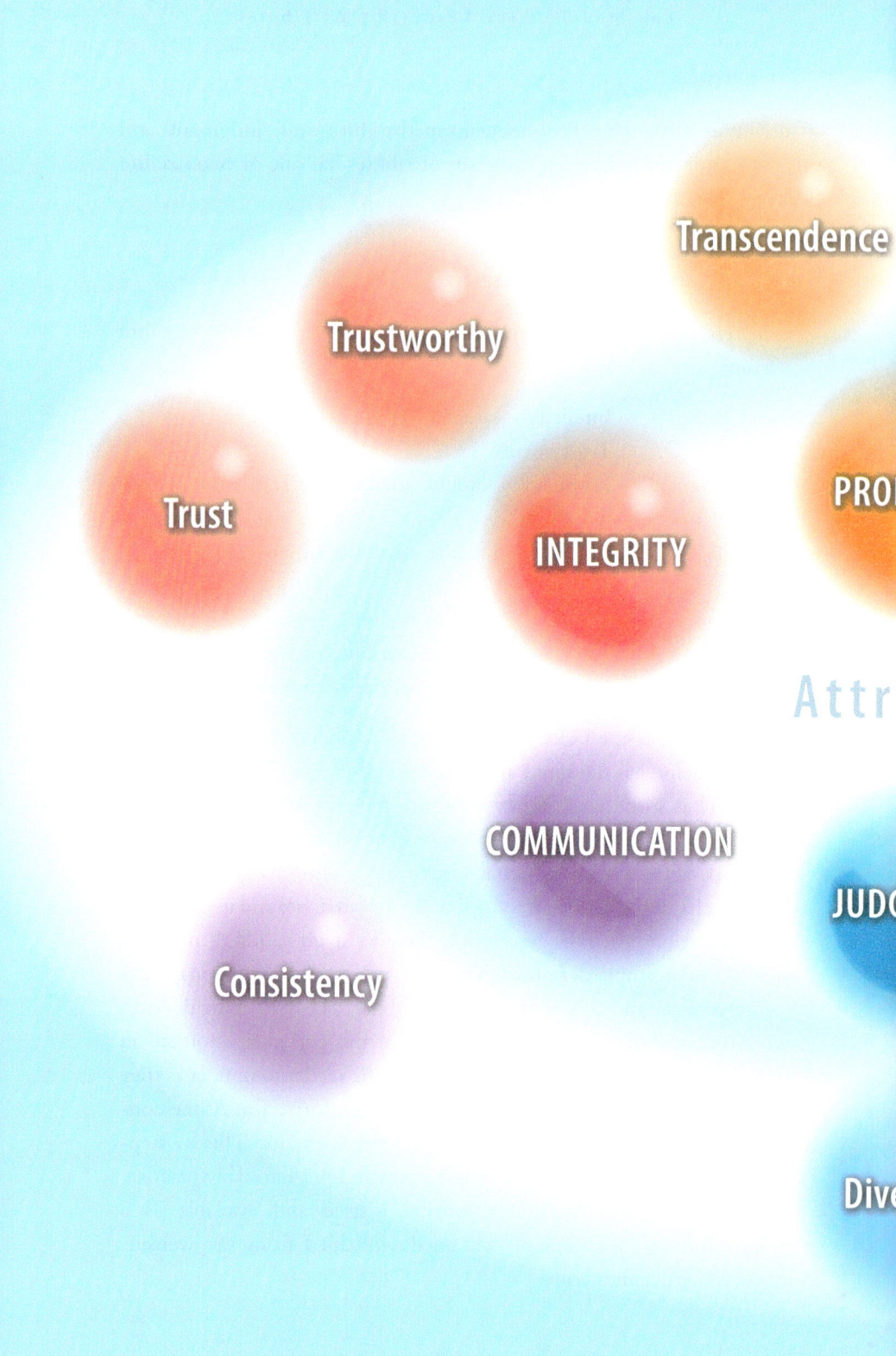

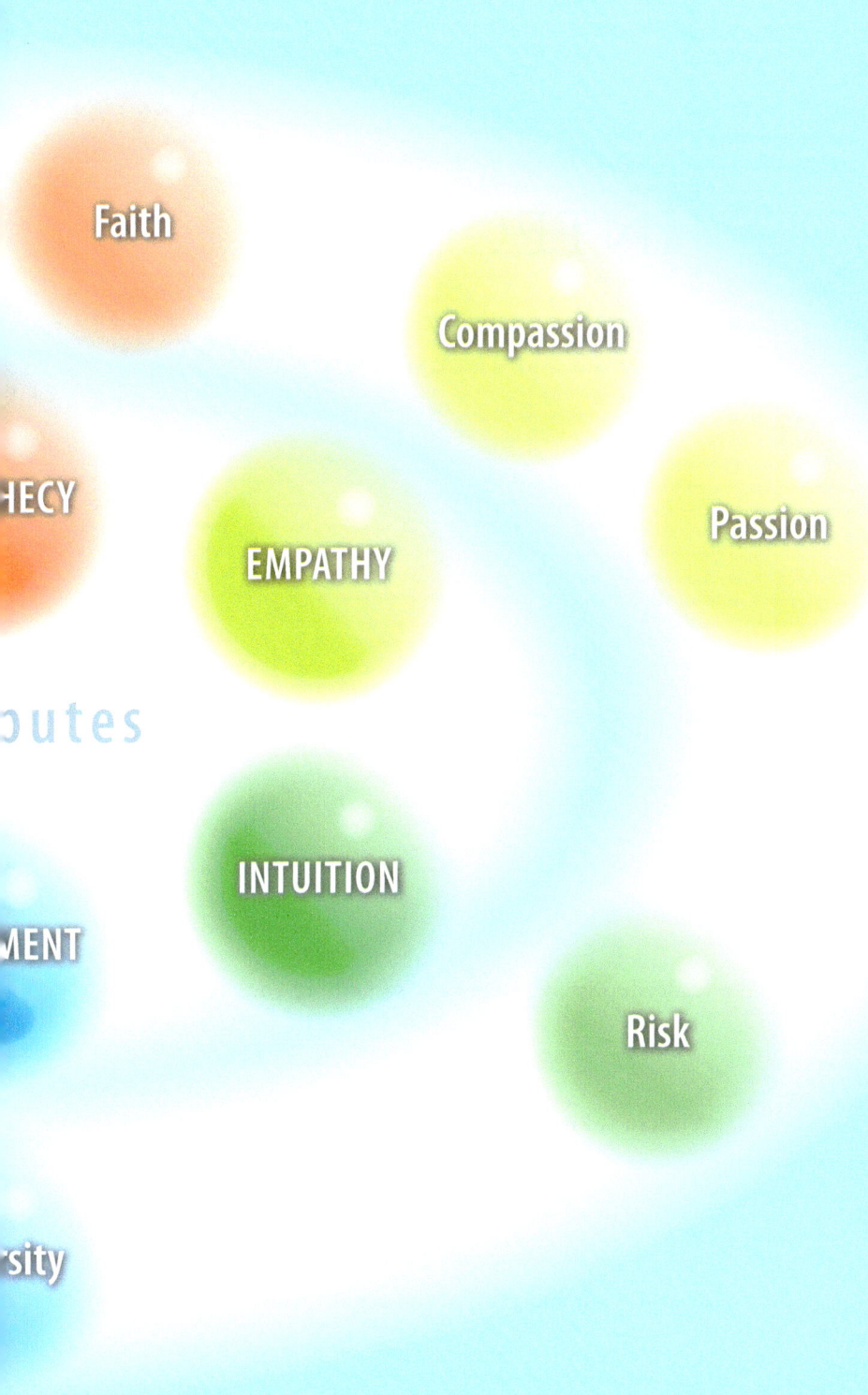

Chapter 4

INTEGRITY

with the satellite attributes of
Trust and **Trustworthy**

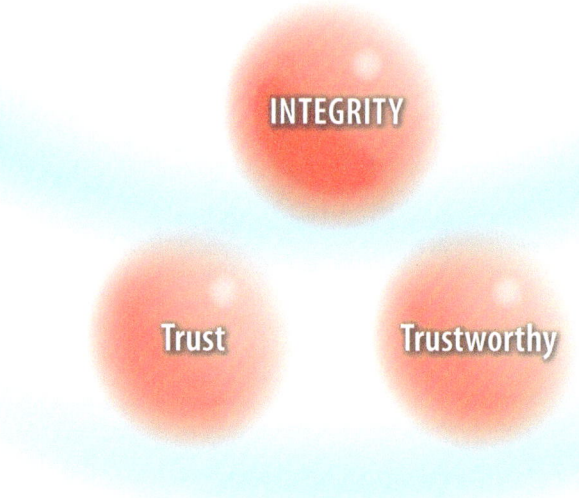

Like leadership itself, integrity is something you are,
not something you do.

John C. Bowling

Wisdom is knowing the right path to take;
integrity is taking it.

M. H. McKee

Motto – 'become' yourself

Symbol – yin and yang ... the way of truth

Integrity

Integrity is being whole and honest. It is found in the quiet recesses of the heart and soul. Integrity is nurtured by the time one spends reflecting upon personal principles and values, then discovering how these are best expressed in the living of life. Success may come and go in your life, but your integrity, whether you have it or not, will last a long time in the minds of others. Integrity should be cherished and protected forever.

The Leadership Attributes of *Trust* and *Trustworthy* are the satellite attributes of *Integrity*. These are discussed within this chapter.

A person of significant integrity was Abraham Lincoln. Before he became President of the United States, Lincoln spent 20 years as an Illinois lawyer. There are countless recorded cases of Lincoln not accepting money from people who owed him for his services. Once a man sent him $25, but Lincoln sent him back ten of it, saying he was being too generous. He was known at times to convince his clients to settle their issue out of court, saving them a lot of money, and earning himself nothing. These are examples of his honesty, which led people – friend and foe – to acknowledge Lincoln as a man of the highest integrity.

One of the well-known stories is that of an old woman in dire poverty, the widow of a revolutionary soldier, who was charged $200 to receive her $400 pension. Lincoln sued the pension agent and won the case for the old woman. He didn't charge her for his services and, in fact, paid her hotel bill and gave her money to buy a ticket home!

There is a very 'unwise' saying that unfortunately dominates so much of people's actions in the fast pace of our current world – 'the end justifies the means.' There are people who will lie in order to achieve their end goal. Every time we lie to satisfy our own needs we lose integrity.

Here is another saying: 'the journey is what is important not the end point.' In other words, what you experience along the way of life is most important, and it is the lessons that you take from those experiences and how you use them to benefit humankind that is 'the priceless gift you give.' It is the gift that strengthens your personal integrity.

Here is a slightly different slant on honesty and integrity. This is a fable with a hint of wisdom.[1]

A Wise Fable

'The trouble with the world,' said the Master with a sigh, 'is that human beings refuse to grow up.'

'When can a person be said to have grown up?' asked the disciple.

'On the day he does not need to be lied to about anything.'

As you reflect upon the attribute of integrity, review the following questions and jot down your thoughts. In doing so, you are engaging in a practice that will enrich your personal integrity.

1. Why is integrity an important attribute for a person to develop within themselves? As a leader?
2. What do you value most in life? List these.
3. Why do you value these? Give examples/stories.
4. What is/are your principle/s in life? What are the things you hold most dear? (As a guide, look back at your answer to question 2.)
5. Can you give an example of when you paid a price to maintain integrity? For example, have you ever been honest with a friend and lost the friendship because of it?
6. Can you remember a time when you were forced to make an unpopular decision? Describe a time when it was important for you to 'take a stand' at work? At home?
7. Can you name a person who you believe has outstanding integrity? (Someone famous and then someone not so famous? A friend?)

Gandhi is a person who displayed great integrity. There are numerous stories of his integrity. Some stories relate to his dealings with government officials and others show his connection to the common person. Several of these stories, which demonstrate Gandhi's integrity and humility, can be found in this book.

Integrity

My Life is My Message – Mahatma Gandhi

Gandhi was not only a political and spiritual leader, he was a great teacher and a great model. Everything he did embodied what he believed. He did not need speeches or 'staged' events to get his message heard.

When he arrived in India, Gandhi spent a great deal of time travelling, visiting and meeting the people. Once, while Gandhi's train was pulling slowly out of a station, a reporter ran up to him and asked Gandhi for a message he could take back to his people. Gandhi replied, 'My life is my message.' Over the next few days, those words were headlines in many papers around the world.

Numerous studies support integrity as being one of the most significant attributes in leadership. A study of more than ten years' duration with 15,000 managers worldwide discovered that integrity was the attribute most highly regarded in a leader.[2] This finding was supported through the results of a study that explored the perceptions, thoughts and feelings of school leaders who are actively engaged in the establishment of schools as moral communities.[3]

From the participants' responses about integrity, several key concepts emerged. These were:

- authenticity
- modelling
- relationships.

Authenticity means being believable. It implies to be authentic in what you say and how you act. Modelling implies practising what you preach, setting an example for others to follow, and, most importantly, being authentic in the process. In the building of community, relationships should be formed with authenticity, trust and hope.

People's interest is raised when they believe in the integrity of another. They sense the authenticity of a person, as seen through modelling and within the relationships they build.

In a study on Leadership Attributes, out of a possible 15 attributes, every participant placed integrity as one of the six most significant attributes required for establishing a moral community. In most cases, integrity was ranked first or second.[4]

One participant said:

> A 'moral' community is one that has integrity and authenticity. I believe there are many truths. The truth is very problematic – there are many truths and many paths to the truth. The challenge is to be authentic about how you respond to those truths. I mean you have to be honest and open about all those things I talked about before (challenging people in a caring and affirming manner). (Participant 9)

Participants spoke of the need for community members and, in particular, leaders to be upfront and honest in order to build the aura of authenticity:

> You may not agree with everything they do, but if they are upfront, honest and integrity is vital (to them) – they are going to be good leaders. (Participant 1)

Several writers in the field believe authenticity should emanate from the practices and actions of a leader (Bezzina, Burford & Duignan, 2007; McGahey, 2002; Starratt, 2005).[5] In this way, authentic relationships are built, nurtured and lead to the formation of communities that are essentially moral or good (Bezzina, 2012; Bowling, 2011; McGahey, 2000, 2002; Sergiovanni, 1996; Starratt, 2012).[6]

Several participants commented:

> Once you get into a leadership position you really do realise that integrity is quite important. (Participant 4)

> You don't get anywhere as a leader if you don't have integrity. (Participant 3)

To model, to lead by example and to practise what you preach echoed continuously throughout the interviews. In this way, you encourage relationships that are authentic and lead to building of community within the workplace, wider community and in the home.

Duty Roster – Mahatma Gandhi

Before going to India, Gandhi established an ashram in South Africa. He would do the weekly duty roster. Gandhi would place himself on toilet duty more than anyone else. People noticed this and his wife got upset and asked him why he rostered himself on that particular duty so much. His reply was that a leader must learn to serve and be a servant to his people - to be willing to work as they do. He would ask of no-one what he himself was not prepared to do. Thus, Gandhi developed the ability to empathise with others and he did this with great integrity.

Another man who showed great integrity in a situation where he had much to lose by being honest is Ruben Gonzalez.[7]

Match Point – Ruben Gonzalez

Playing in his first professional racquetball tournament, Ruben Gonzalez made it through to the finals. At match point, he had the opportunity to take out the championship when a erroneous call was made in his favour. He spoke up, advising the officials that his shot was out and so play continued. Eventually, he lost the match.

However, his honesty, which displayed great integrity, did not go unnoticed. The next issue of a leading racquetball magazine featured Gonzalez on its cover. The editorial spoke of the significance of the moment and Gonzalez's sportsmanship.

Now! All this is fine as a model, but what about the times when a leader has to take someone aside to discuss their faults. This situation has the potential to explode.

Being honest with a person, and having to be critical at times, is not an easy task – particularly for those of us who realise we too are not so perfect. We make mistakes that will cause others to criticise us. And then there is the unknown! How will the person take the criticism?

Will they get upset, storm out or become your enemy and begin to undermine your position? How can we overcome this potentially disastrous situation?

There is a possible solution and it is this: reveal your own good and bad points/faults openly and honestly.

In any situation where criticism has the potential for conflict, always start with your own faults. Talk about your own mistakes and play them up if you have to. 'Show and tell' your mistakes and, most importantly, explain how you have learnt from them. Hopefully your actions will start a life-giving dialogue, which will result in the formation of a trusting relationship.

There is another beautiful story of Gandhi that displays his integrity in the simplicity of his truth. This true story is an adaptation of the version in Blaine Lee's book, *The Power Principle*.[8]

The Sugar Story – Mahatma Gandhi

At one of the large gatherings convened so that Gandhi could address the people, a mother seized the opportunity to have the great sage teach her son a lesson. The little boy was extremely partial to sugar. The following is a scripted version of the event.

The mother asked Gandhi to tell the boy that too much sugar was not good for his teeth and his diet.

Gandhi looked at the child and his mother, then harshly replied, 'I cannot tell him that!'

He proceeded to walk away. After a moment's reflection, he turned and said, 'But you may bring him back in one month's time.'

The woman was frustrated, as she thought Gandhi would support her in her efforts to ensure her child ate wisely. Nonetheless, in a month's time she returned with her son, not really knowing what to expect. They had travelled some distance on both occasions.

Upon seeing them, Gandhi knew exactly who they were. He knelt down and beckoned the child to him. Gracefully, he smiled at the boy and wisely he said, 'Do not eat sugar! It is not good for you!' Gandhi hugged the child and passed him back to his mother.

The mother was grateful but asked, 'Why did you not tell my son this weeks ago?'

Gandhi sighed and replied, 'Four weeks ago I was still eating sugar!'

Gandhi would not ask of others what he himself was not prepared to do. As he constantly said, 'Ask only what you would do.'

This can be simply expressed as:

> The power of example is found
> in the simplicity of its truth.
>
> ~Vicky McGahey~

And the final quote for this attribute:

> To show integrity is simple.
> Just be who you are, warts and all.
>
> ~Vicky McGahey~

> **Attribute in Reflective Action**
> **INTEGRITY**
>
> *How can we build integrity into our daily lives?*
> ***Simply ...***
> Be honest, truthful and do not lie
> ***Also***
> Do not pretend to be who you are not
> ***And***
> Reflect and remain steadfast in the one you have become
> ***Then***
> Be who you are – past, present and future

After significant analysis of the attributes, the following satellite attributes were found to be directly related to the key Leadership Attribute of *Integrity*:

- Trust
- Trustworthy.

Trust in the context of this attribute is to be trusting of another. And, being *Trustworthy* is to be worthy of another's trust. Honesty builds integrity, which, in turn, creates trust. Leaders need to practise openness and see themselves as being worthy of a person's trust. These satellite attributes are discussed in this chapter.

Integrity

Trust

(the willingness to trust)

Trust is like paper. Once it's crumpled
it can't be perfect again.

Unknown

The best way to find out if you can trust
somebody is to trust them.

Ernest Hemingway

Trust is the key to truth; Truth is the key to trust.

Cassandra Eason

Motto – 'become' yourself

Symbol – yin and yang ... the way of truth

To trust is to take a leap of faith. It is the willingness to trust that is essential. If you do not show a willingness to trust, how can you expect to be trusted? As Stephen Covey states 'trust is the highest form of human motivation. It brings out the very best in people.'[9]

Trust and hope walk hand-in-hand together on the tightrope above a gorge. When we trust someone, we do so in the hope they will not let us down. Trust and hope inspire us to move on ... to take the next step. Without hope, we can see no future and then trust is insignificant.

The following story has a subtle but poignant point.[10]

The Bridge Crossing – Little Girl and Father

A little girl and her father were crossing a bridge. The father was a little nervous, so he asked his little daughter to hold his hand, saying 'I don't want you to fall into the river.'

The little girl replied, 'No, Dad. You hold my hand.'

The father stopped and looked at his daughter, puzzled. 'What's the difference?' he asked her.

'There's a big difference,' replied the little girl. 'If I hold your hand and something happens to me, chances are that I may let your hand go. But if you hold my hand, I know for sure that no matter what happens, you will never let my hand go.'

It is not what ties us together (money, job and position) that counts. It is the bonds we make with each other through friendship and relationships. For the little girl, it was the bond of her father's love.

Often we are faced with things, people or opportunities that seem too good to be true ... and doubt creeps in. That is why 'honesty is the best policy.'

There is a valuable lesson to be learnt from this next story from researchers at Cleveland State University.[11]

Credibility Through Honesty

In the mid-1980s, researchers at Cleveland State University made a startling discovery. They conducted an experiment by creating two fictitious job candidates – David and John. The candidates had identical resumes and letters of reference. The only difference was that John's letter included the sentence, 'Sometimes, John can be difficult to get along with.'

They showed the resumes to a number of personnel directors. Which candidate did the personnel directors overwhelmingly prefer? Surprisingly, it was difficult-to-get-along-with John.

The researchers concluded the criticism of John made the praise of John more believable. Admitting John's failing actually helped sell John. Admitting flaws gives you more credibility – a key to selling.

As you reflect upon the attribute of trust consider the following questions and jot down your thoughts. In doing so, you are engaging in a practice that will enrich your personal integrity (trust).

1. Why is trust an important attribute for a person to develop within themself? As a leader?
2. What does trust have to do with building relationships? Give examples/stories.
3. What is the relationship between trust and vulnerability? When was the last time you trusted another? Did it work out OK?
4. Can you trust someone you fear? Why? Why not?
5. Can you respect someone you do not trust, and can you trust someone you do not respect?
6. How willing are you to show you trust another before expecting them to trust you? Give examples/stories.
7. What 'flaws', if any, are you prepared to admit too?
8. Can others count on you? Give examples/stories.
9. What does trust have to do with the quality of someone's character? Why?
10. What place does 'hope' have in this attribute?

The Leadership Attributes Study revealed that trust is deep within the human psyche.[12] Trust ... well, you would like to trust your leaders.

> It is a kind of variable-quality trust – it really depends on to what extent you think the leader is in the game for his or her own benefit. (Participant 4)

> We all make mistakes – the willingness to trust even when we have made a mistake is something we don't do often enough. Though, it is something I try to do ... I would find it very difficult to do this (be willing to trust) without knowing that I am trustworthy – there is a tension. (Participant 3)

So, what does the above comment say about the old lady in the following story?[13] Who should trust whom?

The Old Lady and the Hearing Aid

An old lady had a hearing aid fitted, hidden underneath her hair. A week later she returned to the doctor for her check-up.

'It's wonderful - I can hear everything now,' she reported very happily to the doctor.

'And is your family pleased too?' asked the doctor.

'Oh, I haven't told them yet,' said the old lady, 'And I've changed my will twice already.'

The old lady has a tactical advantage over her family and one she was obviously not willing to share, but is this the correct way to behave? Isn't she deceiving her family? Is this right? To behave deceptively? Mind you, does the old lady have a just reason? What about the family who are maybe saying things about her that they believe she cannot hear? The story revealed the reason 'why' people do not trust one another — we are so concerned that someone is trying to get the better of us and cheat us. There is a wise motto that states: 'you should always forgive but never forget.'

Remember:

> Those who do not show a willingness to
> trust others cannot expect to be trusted.
>
> ~Vicky McGahey~

And:

> Trust those you believe in often;
> trust in yourself always.
>
> ~Vicky McGahey~

Attribute in Reflective Action
TRUST

How can we build trust into our daily lives?

Simply ...

Trust your inner voice - your inner knowing and feeling

Also

Give your heart to a friend

And

Trust others before you expect them to trust you,
always with hope in your heart

Then

Create trusting and trustworthy relationships,
built upon a foundation of hope

The following satellite attribute of *Trustworthy* speaks for itself.

Trustworthy

(worthy of trust)

> You cannot expect to be trusted
> unless you are willing to trust.
>
> **Vicky McGahey**

> To be trusted is a greater compliment
> than being loved.
>
> **George MacDonald**

Motto – 'become' yourself

Symbol – yin and yang ... the way of truth

To be worthy of another's trust you must first show that you trust them. Those who do not show a willingness to trust others cannot expect to be trusted. It is a double-edged sword and trust is a two-way street.

A leader should be the first to offer a hand in trust. The leader will need to communicate openly with others in order to be worthy of another person's trust. Within a community, the followers need to believe that the leader will make judgments based upon competence and values rather than self-interest.[14]

A leader should make explicit their personal principles and values to others. Within a community, this should be done continuously, with passion and sincerity. In this way, leaders are seen to be authentic. To be worthy of trust, a leader should be authentic – 'What you see is what you get.'

Ultimately, the best in people is what is needed to encourage authenticity and lasting relationships built upon the foundations of trust. Sometimes all that is required for the 'very best' to reveal itself is time – the time given when leaders suspend their judgment. The gift of time can be powerful – one that builds trusting relationships that last a lifetime.

As you reflect upon the attribute of trustworthy, consider the following questions, and jot down your thoughts. In doing so, you are engaging in a practice that will enrich your personal integrity (trustworthy).

1. Why is being trustworthy an important attribute for a person to develop within themselves? As a leader?
2. What has it got to do with relationship building? Give examples/stories.
3. What makes a person trustworthy? What do you look for in someone so that you know you can trust them? Give examples/stories.
4. What can you do to get others to see you as being worthy of their trust? Do you keep your promises? Do you do the right thing? Are you dependable? Give examples/stories.
5. How are the attributes of trust and trustworthy related?
6. What is the place of truth and of being truthful when it comes to being worthy of another's trust?
7. What advice would you give to someone who wants to earn back your trust?

As previously stated, to be worthy of trust you must first be trusting – be willing to show trust in another. Trust and trustworthy are very much related. They are the yin and yang of all relationships. The following is a story of trust and trustworthy.[15]

Keith Murdoch Oration - Lachlan Murdoch

To be worthy of trust and to trust in another was highlighted in the story Lachlan Murdoch told about his grandfather during a talk on freedom of speech and freedom of the press. His grandfather was a journalist who reported on the fighting at Gallipoli. Keith Murdoch wrote a personal letter to Andrew Fisher, the Australian Prime Minister, describing the plight of the troops and the horrific situation at the battlefront. In doing so, he went against authority and risked censorship. It is believed that the letter instigated the abandonment of the campaign.

Just as censorship had so clearly hampered the wartime reporting of his grandfather, Lachlan Murdoch, as News Corp co-chairperson, condemned the Abbott Government's new national security laws that could jail journalists for up to ten years for revealing special intelligence operations.

At the Keith Murdoch Oration, Lachlan Murdoch said that the freedom of Australia's press was under threat and had already fallen dramatically by world standards. Quoting statistics, he said:

> **It might surprise you that today Australia ranks 33rd, just behind Belize, on the Freedom House index. Twenty years ago, we ranked 9th.**

Mr Murdoch said the government was frequently asking Australians to trust them when attempting to censor the media by stating, 'we're from the government.' He continued, 'But trust is something that should not be a consideration when restricting our fundamental freedoms. Our freedom of speech and freedom of the press are not things we should blindly entrust to anyone.'

Trust and freedom walk hand in hand.

The Murdoch story is yet another example where trust is seen as a double-edged sword. You must trust another to become worthy of trust.

To be trustworthy implies you are honest. Indeed, a trusting relationship cannot survive without a degree of honesty, even if it is scarce.

The Leadership Attributes Study revealed that people generally like to 'trust their leaders'. (Participant 1).

There is a real need for leaders to be genuine. As previously quoted, one participant clearly stated:

> Willingness to trust/trustworthy are similar. I would find it very difficult to do this (be willing to trust) without knowing that I am trustworthy - there is a tension. (Participant 3)

The following fable demonstrates why you must be honest and truthful in your dealings with others.[16]

Integrity

The Emperor's Seed

An Emperor of an ancient people decided it was time to choose a successor. He was not pleased with his children or the aides in his court. They lacked the integrity, honesty and trust he himself had vigorously displayed during his reign. So he thought up a creative idea to find a young person to take his place. He called all the young people in the kingdom together one day and told them it was time for him to step down and that he was going to choose one of them as the next Emperor. They were all shocked.

'I am going to give each one of you a seed today. One seed. It is a very special seed. I want you to go home, plant the seed, water it and come back here one year from today with what you have grown from this one seed. I will then judge the plants that you bring to me, and the one whose plant I choose will be the next Emperor of the kingdom!'

There was one boy named Ling who was there that day and he, like the others, received a seed. He went home and excitedly told his mother the whole story. She helped him get a pot and some planting soil, and he planted the seed and watered it carefully. Every day he would water it and watch to see if it had grown.

After a few weeks, some of the other youths began to talk about their seeds and the plants that were beginning to grow. Ling kept going home and checking his seed, but nothing ever grew. Three weeks, four weeks, five weeks went by … still nothing.

Six months went by … still there was nothing in Ling's pot. He just knew he had killed his seed. Everyone else had trees and tall plants, but he had nothing. Ling didn't say anything to his friends. He just kept waiting for his seed to grow.

A year finally went by and all the youths brought their plants to the Emperor for inspection. Ling told his mother that he wasn't going to take an empty pot. But she encouraged him to go, and to take his pot, and to be honest about what had happened. Ling felt sick to his stomach, but he knew his mother was right. He took his empty pot to the palace.

When Ling arrived, he was amazed at the variety of plants grown by all the other youths. Ling went to hide at the back. As Ling put his empty pot on the floor, many of the children laughed at him.

When the Emperor arrived, he surveyed the room and greeted the young people. 'Today, one of you will be appointed the next Emperor!'

He walked around and smiled, 'My, what great plants, trees and flowers you have grown.' But he seemed disappointed. Then he asked, 'Did anyone's seed not grow?'

Everyone turned and looked at Ling. The Emperor saw Ling and his empty pot. He ordered his guards to bring him to the front. Ling was terrified. When Ling got to the front, the Emperor asked his name. 'My name is Ling,' he replied. Some of the others started to get a little nervous and some laughed and made fun of Ling. The Emperor asked everyone to quieten down. He looked at Ling, and then announced to the crowd, 'Behold your new Emperor! His name is Ling!' Ling couldn't believe it.

'But how can this be?' asked Ling. 'My seed did not even grow? Me ... as Emperor? I think not!'

The Emperor smiled at Ling and said, 'One year ago today, I gave everyone here a seed. I told everyone to take the seed, plant it, water it, and bring it back to me today. But I gave everyone boiled seeds that would not grow.'

Ling instantly felt his spirits rise. His mother was right. It was almost as if she knew.

'All of you, except Ling,' stated the Emperor, 'have brought me trees and plants and flowers. When you found that the seed would not grow, you substituted another seed for the one I gave you. Ling was the only one with the courage and honesty to bring me a pot with my seed in it. Therefore, he is the one who will be the new Emperor!'

Therefore, seek ways to display trustworthiness – to reveal that you are worthy of another's trust ... but remember to show you can also trust in others.

To be trusted is power, for others will follow.
~Vicky McGahey~

> **Attribute in Reflective Action**
> **TRUSTWORTHY**
>
> *How can we build trustworthy into our daily lives?*
>
> **Simply ...**
>
> Never lie
>
> **Also**
>
> Always show mercy
>
> **And**
>
> Surround yourself with those you trust and become worthy of their trust
>
> **Then**
>
> Be trustworthy

As previously stated, to be worthy of trust you must first be trusting – be willing to show trust in another. Trust and trustworthy are very much related. They are the yin and yang of all relationships.

Here are some extra questions to reflect upon related to integrity, trust and trustworthy. They are concerned with lying – Oh! The lies we do tell!

1. What are white lies? Give examples of the ones you have told? Be brave here. Be honest here. Why did you tell them?
2. Some people say that simply avoiding the truth isn't really a lie. What do you think?
3. What is the biggest lie you've ever told? Would you do it again? Why or why not?
4. Have you ever lied to fit in? Did it help you fit in? If not, what happened?
5. Have you ever told a lie to someone you care about? How did that feel?

To model, to lead by example and to practise what you preach is echoed continuously throughout studies and in the literature on leadership. Indeed, the development of a community can only begin when the leaders behave with integrity and therefore display authenticity.

In the Leadership Attributes Study, participants revealed many interesting insights.[17]

> However, integrity alone is not enough. You can have tremendous integrity but the organisation is not actually going anywhere. (Participant 10)

Therefore, a leader needs to develop a second key Leadership Attribute that requires a person to be prophetic and visionary. It is an attribute that challenges people to be the best they can be. Hence, the attribute of *Prophecy*.

Chapter 5

PROPHECY

with the satellite attributes of
Transcendence and **Faith**

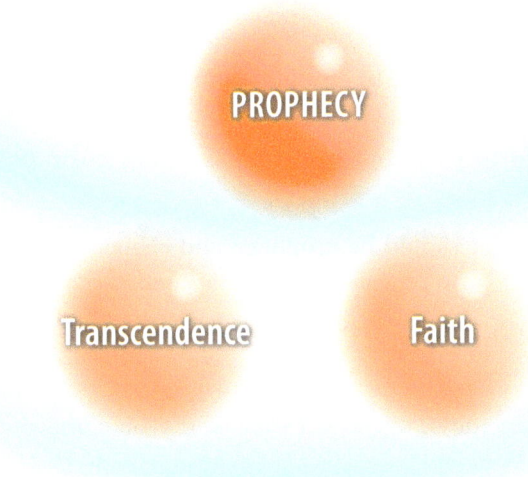

You must do the things you think you cannot do.
Eleanor Roosevelt

The future belongs to those who believe
in the beauty of their dreams.
Eleanor Roosevelt

Community needs leadership that can 'touch the future'
by reaching beyond reality to engage people in reflection,
thought and action towards new possibilities.
Vicky McGahey

Motto – be prepared to make a stand

Symbol – key

Prophecy has long been seen as the work of prophets and mystics – those mysterious and inspired people who would state the reality of now and tell stories of a possible future. But in today's fast-paced world, with our need for instant joy and gratification, as individuals we have become the prophets of our own future. In a world that experiences suffering and sorrow on a grand scale, now, more than ever, we need to be prophets of hope.

The Leadership Attributes of *Transcendence* and *Faith* are the satellite attributes of *Prophecy*. These are discussed within this chapter.

From a leadership perspective, prophecy is associated with vision and mission. A leader needs to dream a vision that can become a 'shared vision' – one that will motivate others to engage in the challenges set before them. To be prophetic is to be challenging ... or the message is lost.

> A leader should be prophetic and challenging.
> Be prepared to make a stand.
>
> **Vicky McGahey**[1]

As Stephen Covey reminds us, a leader should begin a journey with the end in mind, but not fearful of the outcome or the end product. Leaders need to remain self-motivated, confident and ready to articulate their vision (prophecy) of the future for their community.[2]

As you reflect upon the attribute of prophecy, consider the following questions and jot down your thoughts. In doing so, you are engaging in a practice that will enrich your personal prophecy.

1. Why is prophecy an important attribute for a person to develop within themself? As a leader?
2. Have there been times when you predicted a certain outcome in a relationship? Good or bad? Give examples/stories.
3. What are the qualities a person needs to make sound prophecies (predictions of possible outcomes)?
4. Why should you challenge yourself as a prophet of hope?
5. In what ways can you challenge yourself as a prophet of hope?

6. Think back to a time when you made a stand and held firm for something you believed in? What happened? Did you act upon it?
7. What does it mean to be prophets of hope and prophets of our own future? Why is this important? How can we live it?

There are numerous examples of well-known leaders – past and present – who were considered prophetic. Through their thoughts and actions they challenged us to become better people. These include Nelson Mandela, Mahatma Gandhi, Mother Teresa, Mary MacKillop, Jesus of Nazareth, Dalai Lama, Elizabeth I, Socrates, Noam Chomsky and Bertrand Russell. The list is endless. Prophetic leaders are also found in community. These include leaders such as teachers, not-for-profit and local group organisers and family members. They help us to seek out greener pastures as did the shepherds of old as they led their flock.[3] We should never be too fearful of the challenge that lies ahead – just cautious.

The following story is about a person who personified just what it means to challenge others. She would use her powerful persona to get others to err on the side of what is right and just.

A Prophet of Hope – Eleanor Roosevelt

Eleanor Roosevelt was the wife of wartime President Franklin D. Roosevelt. She once said of herself:

> About the only value the story of my life may have is to show that one can, even without any particular gifts, overcome obstacles that may seem insurmountable ... I have had only three assets: I was keenly interested, I accepted every challenge and every opportunity to learn more, and I had great energy and self-discipline.[4]

In 1945, Franklin D. Roosevelt died and Harry S. Truman became President. Within 18 months, President Truman had invited Eleanor to chair a committee to write the Declaration of Human Rights.

The Declaration of Human Rights was a lifelong journey for Eleanor. It was fitting that by the end of a long career as the First Lady during her husband's presidential term, a politician in her own right, a lobbyist, and as a social justice advocate, she stood before the United Nations General Assembly at the Palais de Chaillot in Paris and gave the opening address for the acceptance of the Declaration of Human Rights by the member nations.

> We stand today at the threshold of a great event both in the life of the United Nations and in the life of mankind. This Universal Declaration of Human Rights may well become the international Magna Carta for all men everywhere ...
>
> This Declaration is based upon the spiritual fact that man must have freedom in which to develop his full stature and through common effort to raise the level of human dignity.[5]

Ten years later, at the 10th Anniversary of the Declaration, she shifted her focus. Her primary message was simple. It spoke not of what only great nations should do, but what each and every one of us should do as individuals. Here is some of what she said:

> Where, after all, do universal human rights begin? In small places, close to home – so close and so small that they cannot be seen on any maps of the world. Yet they are the world of the individual person; the neighbourhood he lives in; the school or college he attends; the factory, farm, or office where he works. Such are the places where every man, woman and child seeks equal justice, equal opportunity, equal dignity without discrimination. Unless these rights have meaning there, they have little meaning anywhere. Without concerted citizen action to uphold them close to home, we shall look in vain for progress in the larger world ...[6]

Eleanor spoke of social justice beginning in the home. She, like Gandhi, believed that we ourselves need to become the change we wish to see in the world. Eleanor Roosevelt's words still challenge us today to live out her prophecy and her dream. She also once said: 'The future belongs to those who believe in the beauty of their dreams.'[7]

The Leadership Attributes Study found that prophecy is a key attribute when associated with vision and mission.[8]

If there is a spark of genius in the leadership function at all, it must be in the transcending ability, a kind of magic, to assemble out of a

Prophecy

variety of images, signals, forecasts and alternatives – a clearly articulated vision of the future that is at once single, easily understood, clearly desirable, and energising. (Bennis & Nanus, 1985)[9]

The participants' responses surrounded several key concepts for prophecy as a Leadership Attribute. These are:

- vision (and mission)
- wisdom
- justice
- passion.

When speaking of a fellow colleague, one participant noted:

[She is] confident of her own place in life and able to articulate a vision that was large enough for others to share and then recreate their own stories. (Participant 6)

A vision can become 'shared' through changes made in open dialogue with the members of a community.

There is a need for dialogue that will 'draw to your attention to things that you might need to think about ... questioning and challenging what people think.' (Participant 5)

The participants of the study were able to describe the leadership attributes and practices required for establishing a community that is essentially a moral community. For example:

He brings an incredible moral depth to his leadership and he is wise. He brings great wisdom. He is very intelligent and I think this is really important for moral leadership to have really intelligent people who are bigger than the little scenes, who have a bigger frame of reference than the actual little enterprise you are dealing with now. People like him, because he will take a stance for what is right. They are inspiring, so they really encourage people to keep looking for the good of the community and the people. So I think he is a good example of a moral leader. (Participant 8)

Participants spoke of leaders challenging members of the community to be voices that speak out about issues such as social justice and the protection of the needy and most vulnerable of the community. They believed 'a community' (as a moral community) should 'side with the least powerful in the community or take the side of those who are most vulnerable.' (Participant 3)

This view is reflected in the following participant's comment:

> We are as good a group or community to the extent to which we treat the most disadvantaged person or how we relate to the most disadvantaged member of our community and that will give you a sense of how really moral we are in our actions. I think that is where it really counts. In terms of implications for leaders of community – it is how we reflect upon this. (Participant 8)

When leaders challenge the community to take action on social issues, a growth in moral reasoning begins. Wenniger, in a 1997 article, suggested 'growth from one moral reasoning level to the next normally results from expanding awareness of social issues (global) and one's place in the larger world.'[10]

One participant in the study spoke of leaders being prophetic and challenging with passion in their hearts. Therefore, 'leaders should make explicit that which is implicit through their passion and commitment.' (Participant 9)

Through this passion, leaders are able to 'get others engaged in things, because they see what the leader is saying is of greater value than what they are doing.' (Participant 4)

Participants are able to dream a vision that will motivate others to engage actively in the challenges of the vision that their leader(s) put before them. This can present its own challenges for 'being able to continue and work with that passion even when things get tough requires continuous energy.' (Participant 3)

Thousands of studies have been conducted over the years to determine what motivates people to work. Many of these have discovered that money, good working conditions and fringe benefits are not the prime motivators for good work.

In his timeless book *How to Win Friends & Influence People*, Dale Carnegie tells a true story of motivation.[11]

The Mill – Charles M. Schwab

Charles M. Schwab was the owner of a steel mill. At a very young age, he began dealing with his staff in innovative ways. He would set challenges for his workers to encourage 'healthy competition' that stimulated growth in productivity.

Schwab had a mill manager whose workers were not producing their quota of work.

'How is it,' Schwab asked him, 'that a manager as capable as you can't make this mill turn out what it should?'

'I don't know,' the manager replied. 'I've coaxed the men, I've pushed them, I've even sworn.'

This conversation took place at the end of the day, and the night shift were about to come in. Schwab asked for a piece of chalk and turning to the nearest man, he asked how any 'heats' they had made that day – 'six' was the reply. Without another word, Schwab chalked a big figure '6' on the floor.

When the night shift came in, they asked about the '6' on the floor. The day shift told them the boss had been in and asked how many 'heats' they had made – it was six.

The next morning, Schwab walked though the factory. The night shift had scribbled out the '6' and placed a bigger '7'.

When the day shift reported for work the next morning, they saw a big '7' on the floor. So the night shift thought they were better than the day shift, did they? Well, they would show the night shift a thing or two! The crew pitched in with enthusiasm, and when they quit that night they left behind them an enormous, swaggering '10'. Things were stepping up. Shortly, this mill was turning out more work than any other mill in the plant.

Charles Schwab simply stimulated competition. This was done not in a sordid, money-grabbing manner, but by encouraging the desire to excel.

The desire to excel! The challenge! Throwing down the gauntlet! An infallible way of appealing and to stir the spirit of the people into action!

The one major factor that motivates people to work is the work itself. If the work is exciting and interesting, then people look forward to doing it and are motivated to do a good job.

We look for the chance for self-expression from an early age. As Sir Ken Robinson teaches us in several of his TED talks and related books, we are born into this world very creative and we spend most of the rest of our life being taught how to lose this skill.[12] There is also an inherent need to prove our worth, to excel and to be part of something worthwhile. The desire to excel and the desire for recognition are very human traits that have led to many great works, discoveries and innovations.

As Aristotle once said: 'Pleasure in the job puts perfection in the work.'

Rotary – a community-based, non-government organisation – has a saying that helps remind a club that it needs to constantly involve every one of its members: A happy Rotarian is a working Rotarian.

Being prophetic is more than dreaming a vision for the future. It is also the lifting of awareness of our connectivity to each other, to our world and the universe. There are certain cultures that have been aware of this facet of existence for hundreds of years – one such example is the Fijian culture, as demonstrated in the following story.

Bula! – The Fijian Connection

In Fiji, when you pass a person – whether you know them or not – you greet them with 'Bula!' (pronounced boo-lah!), and, in return, they greet you. You do this as you walk the street. All day long, even if you pass the same person within a short time, you say 'Bula!'

The literal meaning of 'Bula' is 'life', and when used as a greeting it implies wishes for continued good health. For Fijians, there is no such thing as passing someone and not acknowledging your moment of connection, not letting others know of their effect on you and seeing yours on them. For Fijians, connection is natural, just the way the world is made. The Fijians are aware of a basic human law - that we all influence one another. We are part of each other's reality.

The Chaos Theory is an accepted principle of science that acknowledges this connection. In 1972, meteorologist Edward Lorenz theorised that a butterfly flapping its wings in Brazil could cause a tornado in Texas.[13]

As the motto for this attribute states – to be prophetic is being prepared to make a stand. It is to be visionary and mission-driven, which is a call to action. Your passion and sense of justice will prevail and wisdom will be your reward.

> A graceful vision of a grace-filled mission
> is a call to action.
> ~Vicky McGahey~

> **Attribute in Reflective Action**
> **PROPHECY**
>
> *How can we build prophecy into our daily lives?*
>
> **Simply ...**
> Dream and believe dreams can come true
>
> **Also**
> Be the prophet of your own future
>
> **And**
> Become the change you wish to see in the world
>
> **Then**
> Be a prophet of hope

After significant analysis of all the attributes, the following satellite attributes were found to be directly related to the key Leadership Attribute of *Prophecy*:

- Transcendence
- Faith.

Transcendence is seeing the context of the Leadership Attributes as a movement to a higher place – either physical or spiritual. *Faith* is a belief in one's self, including the principles, values and beliefs held dear. For many, it is a belief in the unknown, god or a future life after death.

Prophecy

Transcendence

I have a dream.
Martin Luther King, Jr

*Ask not what your country can do for you –
ask what you can do for your country.*
John F. Kennedy

Motto – be prepared to make a stand

Symbol – key

Transcendence is defined by the *Oxford Dictionary* as an existence or experience beyond the normal or physical level. The *Macquarie Dictionary* states it is being beyond matter, and having a continuing existence therefore outside the created world. It is that which is beyond experience.

This attribute was discussed by Bennis and Nanus:[14]

> Transcendence can be described as a kind of magic with
> the ability to bring all aspects of change, dilemma and
> ideas together within a single vision of the future that is
> understandable, desirable and life-giving.

Several writers in the field of leadership speak of 'transcendent leadership'. In their 2008 article, 'Transcendent Leadership: Strategic Leadership in Dynamic Environments,' Crossan, Vera and Nanjad argue that transcendent leadership can provide a framework for the modern strategic leader in the chaotic context of today's world.[15] A transcendent leader will lead from within and that includes leadership of the self, i.e. being self-aware. They will be proactive in developing personal strengths. This is also supported in the research work of Michie and Gooty (2005) on an individual's self-transcendent values.[16]

For me, transcendence means those moments when I rise to another plane of existence. There, I get a sense of 'the knowing' – the instinctive awareness of our place on Earth as it is in heaven. It is purity and perfection, eminence and excellence, goodness and grace.

Being a satellite attribute of prophecy, transcendence is also related to vision. Within this context, transcendence is the development of a clear vision of the future that is energising and desirable. It describes the ability to consider the aspects of change, challenges, dilemmas and ideas. A vision can become 'shared' through open dialogue with others. In this way, the challenges are faced together and the vision becomes one worth living for everyone within a community, organisation or family.

Leaders need to remain self-motivated and ready to articulate their graceful vision of the future. In other words, a leader should use their vision as a motivator and a starting point for the formation of a collective vision that is continually transformed into mission as the winds of change blow. In this sense, a mission is a call to action. Therefore, a leader needs to be prophetic and challenging.

Women such as Mother Teresa and Mary MacKillop had visions that they shared, and through their actions they found guidance and support from others. There will always be hurdles to jump and walls to climb – physically and mentally. It is the manner in which the obstacles are tackled that counts ... a leader should endeavour to do all things graciously – and, as Gandhi often indicated, to leave the outcome in the hands of God.

Today, we are fortunate to have movies that can place alternative realities in front of us visually. The wonderful visual effects never cease to amaze. However, I have often found my own imagination can produce visions and stimulate my senses to a higher level than any visual effect. I also find it easier to believe that I am really there when I dream and use my own imagination.

As you reflect upon the attribute of transcendence, consider the following questions and jot down your thoughts. In doing so, you are engaging in a practice that will enrich your personal prophecy (transcendence).

1. Why is transcendence an important attribute for a person to develop within themself? As a leader?
2. Why should we allow ourselves to dream, to transcend beyond the here and now?
3. Why is an awareness of the ability to transcend important? (In other words, the transcendent essence of becoming fully who you are?)
4. How future-driven are you? Are you mindful of the past while remaining steadfast in the present? Give examples/stories.
5. Name other people (famous or non-famous) who have this transcendent ability? Do they use it for the good of themselves and humankind? Who are those who caused harm to humankind?

There is a story of four rabbis who went to see the Wheel of Ezekiel. This story is a modified version taken from the book *Women Who Run With the Wolves* by Clarissa Pinkola Estés.[17]

The Four Rabbis

Ezekiel was a biblical prophet who had a vision of paradise. In that vision he saw a wheel within a wheel. There are many drawings and painting of this vision. The experience was obviously transformational for Ezekiel. It was the type of sensation and euphoria many of us can only dream of reaching while on Earth.

The Talmudic version of this story has the four rabbis entering paradise to study the heavenly mysteries.

> One night, four rabbis were visited by an angel who awakened them and carried them to the Seventh Vault of the Seventh Heaven. There they beheld the sacred Wheel of Ezekiel.
>
> Somewhere in the descent from Paradise to Earth, one rabbi, having seen such splendour, lost his mind and wandered frothing and foaming until the end of his days. The second rabbi was extremely cynical and said, 'Oh, I just dreamed Ezekiel's Wheel, that was all. Nothing *really* happened.' The third rabbi carried on and on about what he had seen, for he was totally obsessed. He lectured and would not stop with how

> it was all constructed and what it all meant ... and in this way he went astray and betrayed his faith. The fourth rabbi, who was a poet, took a paper in hand and a reed and sat near the window writing song after song praising the evening dove, his daughter in her cradle, and all the stars in the sky. And he lived his life better than before.

How difficult is it, at times, not to be so much in awe that we lose sight of reality? Not to be so cynical that we begin to doubt? Not to be so obsessive that our actions become too extreme?

It would seem the wisest path to take is one of contemplation, reflection and giving of thanks. Then allowing the experience to gradually change you so that you live a better life because of it.

Not too much and not too little. Not too high and not too low. The way of leadership is not found in the extremes but the in-between of the extremes. More often than not it is the middle ground. There may be a high road and a low road but the leader may need to go bush bashing and create a new road that cuts down the middle. It is like a wheel within a wheel – all spinning in harmony.

Rotary International, a not-for-profit organisation, has a wheel within a wheel as its symbol or trademark for an associated, but separate, organisation called Inner Wheel, which was founded by the wives of Rotarians and is traditionally organised by women. Like Rotary, Inner Wheel provides funds and help to those in need.

The Leadership Attributes Study revealed that participants considered that the ability to communicate a transcendent vision was an essential attribute.[18] One participant stated:

> A good leader is capable of transcendence ... of seeing a future that is better, that is achievable, desirable and energising and so on. And be able to articulate that vision in the way that other people want to follow – to be part of this vision. (Participant 3)

Yet another participant commented:

> Transcendence is fine. Transcendence means more than that to me – it is visionary. However, transcendence implies another quality for it encapsulates a few different ideas. One of those

ideas is visionary, one of them is trusting in your intuition and that gives you the ability to transcend the normal – to transcend the day-to-day and have a picture of glory if you like. That is a little bit visionary as well. (Participant 2)

In this sense, transcendence touches at the heart of trust.

The Chosen People – Numbers 32: 13 and 34: 1-2

We develop a belief that there is a deeper meaning in all things in life - even the petty events. All can be used to enrich our lives profoundly.

For example, there is one noted period of biblical history when the people of Israel wandered aimlessly in the desert for 40 years:

> And the Lord's anger was kindled against Israel, and he made them wander in the wilderness for forty years, until all the generation that had done evil in the sight of the Lord had disappeared. (Numbers 32: 13)

They were the chosen people, who were punished by God for the sin of pride. But, through the transcending visions of Moses, they came to believe in the future of their nation and in the compassion of God. And, God did reward them for their loyalty, faith and righteous actions:

> The Lord spoke to Moses, saying 'command the Israelites, and say to them: When you enter the land of Canaan this is the land that shall fall to you for your inheritance (the land of Canaan, defined by its boundaries).' (Numbers 34: 1-2)

Albert Einstein once said: 'The most beautiful thing we can experience is the mysterious. It is the source of all true art and science.' To learn from the mysterious requires us to reflect and listen to the voice within. Einstein spent most of his life as an agnostic, but he saw the value of the unknown and the hope for a better world here and into the next life. He also said: 'Science without religion is lame; religion without science is blind.' Therefore,

Be still, listen and reach beyond.

~Vicky McGahey~

> **Attribute in Reflective Action**
> **TRANSCENDENCE**
>
> *How can we build transcendence into our daily lives?*
>
> **Simply ...**
>
> Dream
>
> **Also**
>
> Dream of a graceful vision,
>
> for a grace-filled mission is a call to action
>
> **And**
>
> Live your dream so that you never
>
> lose sight of the dream
>
> **Then**
>
> Transcend beyond

The next satellite attribute of *Prophecy* is *Faith*.

PROPHECY

Faith

Hold faithfulness and sincerity as first principles.
Confucius, *The Analects of Confucius*

Sometimes the hardest things to believe are
the only things worth believing at all.
E. J. Patten, *Return to Exile*

Motto – be prepared to make a stand

Symbol – key

Faith is a belief in a future. Sometimes that future is not of our own making.

Faith is also the belief in oneself and the principles, values and beliefs one holds dear. A leader can bring people together through faith. This requires getting others to believe in you. And, like the leadership attribute of transcendence, from this gathering of followers, shared principles, values and beliefs can emerge with a clear vision of the future that is both energising and desirable.

The attribute of faith grows with the other 15 Leadership Attributes as they emerge through the actions of a leader. Altogether, they provide hope for the future of a community, organisation and the family.

As you reflect upon the attribute of faith, consider the following questions and jot down your thoughts. In doing so, you are engaging in a practice that will enrich your personal prophecy (faith).

1. Why is faith an important attribute for a person to develop within themself? As a leader?
2. What is faith in oneself? This includes faith in one's abilities; it also includes faith in one's future. Give examples/stories.
3. Do you have faith in yourself? If not, why not?
4. List your principles, values and beliefs (see Chapter 10 and appendices). Start to formulate these.
5. Do you have faith in others? If not, why not?
6. Name some people in whom you have faith.

Faith should not be taken lightly, nor should it be blind to reality, as the following story poignantly demonstrates.[19]

God Will Save Me

This is an old story, told in numerous ways. Still, the message is strong.

There was a terrible storm raging across the inland plains. A flooded river had risen so high that a once-thriving town was now submerged. There had been numerous warnings of the urgency of the situation and people were ordered to evacuate immediately.

A man of faith had heard the warnings but he decided to stay, for he believed that God would save him. 'I trust God. He will not allow me to perish in the storm. He will send a divine miracle to save me.'

Some neighbours came by his house and said to him, 'Come, there is room in our car! We can take you to safety.'

But the man refused, stating boldly, 'I trust in God! He will save me.'

So they left. The waters were rapidly rising and the man had to seek refuge on the second floor of his house. He sat on the windowsill looking out, waiting for God. A man in a canoe came paddling by and cried out, 'Come, I will save you! There is room in my canoe for two.'

The man refused the kind gesture saying, 'My God will save me!'

It was not long before the waters entered through the windows on the second floor. The man had to climb onto his roof. There he waited. Eventually, he heard the sound of a helicopter. 'Ahoy down there,' came the voice from the sky, 'Climb this rope ladder.'

But once again, the man refused the help. He cried out above the noise of the rotors, 'God will save me!'

Eventually, the house broke up in the floodwaters, swept the man away and he drowned. He went to heaven and, upon seeing God, he said, 'I am a religious man and I have prayed to you every day. I put all of my faith in you! Why did you let me drown?'

God recognised the man and said, 'I sent you a warning, I sent you a car, I sent you a canoe and then a helicopter. What more were you looking for?' God smiled and said, 'What the hell are you doing here?'

The religious message is obvious: do not let overzealous faith blind you to reality. God works miracles using nature – people and objects. He will transcend space and time to save you, but it may be through the deeds of others. Therefore, always remain grounded in reality, so that you can see the 'acts of God' as they naturally occur.

From a leadership perspective, the story revealed the need for us to extend our hand to those who trust us and put their faith in us. Then hopefully, in return, they will extend their hand to us.

Many of the participants of the Leadership Attribute Study agreed with the premise that faith is a belief in a future and one that is not necessarily of our own making. They warmed to Gandhi's philosophy that implied you can only do what you can do, the outcome you must leave up to God. This way of looking at faith gives a person 'empowerment of myself, which is guided by my soul' (Participant 2). Another participant said:

> Gandhi took a stand in certain ways ... so should we as leaders ... do not be frightened of the outcome and be willing to take a risk ... that is a form of leadership. (Participant 2)

In her book *Your Personal Renaissance: 12 Steps to Finding Your Life's True Calling,* Diane Dreher wrote on the life and times of the people of the Renaissance.[20] She told the stories of well-known figures of the Renaissance and then folded these into the realities of the here and now. Many people of the time were empowered by a sense of calling or vocation to become the best they could possibly be. They believed that everyone – from kings to commoners – had a calling to greatness and that each of them had been given special talents. Renaissance women and men became the artists, poets, musicians, scientists and political leaders that brought the world out of the Dark Ages and into the era of the Enlightenment.

> Like the Renaissance women and men,
> we too must become people of faith,
> to believe in a destiny within a purpose-filled
> yet unknown universe.
>
> ~Vicky McGahey~

> **Attribute in Reflective Action**
> **FAITH**

How can we build faith into our daily lives?
Simply ...
Breathe! Believe and know you exist
Also
Seek ways to know thyself as you journey
And
Live with hope always in your heart
Then
Believe in yourself

The development of learning for future generations requires leadership that can 'touch the future'. This is leadership that reaches beyond reality to engage people in reflective thought and action towards new possibilities. To achieve this, leaders need to develop a third key Leadership Attribute that requires them to listen and to be empathetic towards others in the community, organisation and the family. Hence, the attribute of *Empathy*.

Chapter 6

EMPATHY

with the satellite attributes of
Compassion and **Passion**

Empathy is a loving silence that has far more power to heal and connect than most well-intentioned words.
Rachel Naomi Remen

Empathy is the art of listening and feeling with compassion and passion.
Vicky McGahey

Motto – listen to feel

Symbol – heart

> The most profound gift you can give
> another person is your empathy.
> It requires you to stop ... listen and feel.
> ~Vicky McGahey~

Effective leaders listen empathetically. Leaders need to increase their empathy by taking the time to listen and immerse themselves in the problems and issues of others. They should show a willingness to communicate openly and honestly. This develops trust and believability in a person's integrity. Such feeling and listening will encourage honest dialogue between people in a community. This could lead to a growth in integrity within individuals and within the whole community.

The Leadership Attributes of *Compassion* and *Passion* are the satellite attributes of *Empathy*. These are discussed within this chapter.

An article by Alexander Lucia argues convincingly for organisational leaders, such as school leaders, to hear what others have to say and to empathise with their issues:[1]

> People perceive a lack of empathy because those around them don't take the time to find out what they're feeling and yes, don't take the time to listen. So these two characteristics – caring and feeling – are very much intertwined.

As you reflect upon the attribute of empathy, review the following questions and jot down your thoughts. In doing so, you are engaging in a practice that will enrich your personal empathy.

1. Why is empathy an important attribute for one to develop within themself? As a leader?
2. Why should we build a culture of empathy? How? Give examples/stories.
3. How is it different from sympathy or pity? Describe how one exercises empathy versus sympathy or pity.
4. How do you remain mindful of the needs of others while ever-mindful of the limitations within yourself (in certain situations)?

5. Who is the most empathetic person you know? How does it make you feel to be around this person?
6. Can you think of a person who showed you empathy in a situation (i.e. being empathetic to you and your plight)?
7. Is there a situation right now? A person who may be in need of your care, kindness and empathy right now? Go to them, regardless!

An example of a person who displayed great empathy as a leader and as a person was Abraham Lincoln. There are several stories about his passion, compassion and great ability to empathise with others. Nonetheless, it was Dale Carnegie who shone the light to reveal the true character of Abraham Lincoln.[2] The following is a rendition formed by the writer based mainly upon Carnegie.

Confederate Escape – Abraham Lincoln

The Battle of Gettysburg was fought in the first days of July 1863, with a great victory for the Union Army, led by General Meade. By 13 July, Meade's forces had chased General Lee and the Confederates to the banks of the Potomac River. On the southern side of the river was the Confederacy and escape.

But the Potomac River was swollen and impassable. Lee and his army were trapped, and it was pouring with rain, so there was no hope of the river waters receding any time soon. Meade knew of Lee's predicament, but he hesitated and telegraphed all manner of excuses to Lincoln as to why he should wait. Meade was certain that Lee could not possibly escape.

Lincoln was beside himself, for he realised that a resounding defeat of the Confederates now could possibly end the war.

Around midnight, a Confederate guard on duty by the river made an interesting observation. Even though it was still raining quite heavily, the waters were starting to drop rapidly. This was because it had stopped raining up river.

He ran to awaken General Lee, who was quick to seize the moment, and the Confederates escaped across the river to freedom. By the next morning, as Meade planned to either attack or arrange a Confederate surrender, he was told of the escape.

Lincoln was furious. Apparent he ranted on and on at the top of his voice throughout the White House. Eventually, he sat down and wrote the following letter to Meade:

My Dear General,

I do not believe you appreciate the magnitude of the misfortune involved in Lee's escape. He was within our easy grasp, and to have closed upon him would, in connection with our other late successes, have ended the war. As it is, the war will be prolonged indefinitely. If you could not safely attack Lee last Monday, how can you possibly do so south of the river, when it can take you very few – no more than two-thirds of the force you then had in hand? It would be unreasonable to expect and I do not expect that you can now affect much. Your golden opportunity is gone, and I am distressed immeasurably because of it.

This is the letter he wrote! The truth is Meade never saw the letter. Lincoln never sent it. It was found among his papers after his death in an envelope marked 'To General Meade from President Lincoln – never sent.'

One could imagine Lincoln sitting back in his chair while looking out on the green, peaceful and safe gardens of the White House and, upon further reflection, thinking 'it is easy for me to sit here and criticise, but if I had seen as much blood as Meade and heard the screams of dying men, maybe I would not be so anxious to attack, and given Meade's cautionary approach to attacking entrenched positions, yes, I would have done just that.'

It appears that Lincoln knew the nature of his general and he was prepared to empathise with him and to make judgment on Meade's inactions based upon the nature and character of Meade and not of himself.

Lincoln, in his second inaugural address stated: 'Judge not, that ye be not judged.'[3]

It turns out that one of Lincoln's techniques was to write letters and never send them. The exercise of writing a letter was to clear his mind and help vent his very strong emotions.

What a powerful strategy for all of us! Have you ever sent a letter or an email and wished you had not? You just wish that you had waited to 'cool down' and let some of the emotion blow free and out of the argument.

Lincoln did send a letter that showed humility and empathy. This is the letter he sent to another general:

> General Howard Washington,
>
> ... A few days having passed, I am now profoundly grateful for what was done, without criticism for what was not done. General Meade has my confidence as a brave and skillful officer, and a true man.

Meade did go to the White House to see Lincoln, and wrote the following to his wife after meeting with the president:

> Yesterday I received an order to repair to Washington, to see the President ... The President was, as he always is, very considerate and kind. He found no fault with my operations, although it was very evident he was disappointed that I had not got a battle out of Lee. He coincided with me that there was not much to be gained by any farther advance; but General Halleck was very urgent that something should be done, but what that something was he did not define. As the Secretary of War was absent in Tennessee, final action was postponed till his return.
>
> General Meade

Lincoln was also known for his belief in 'keeping friends close and your enemies closer.'[4] This practice was first attributed to Sun Tzu, a Chinese general and military strategist around 500BC.[5]

In relation to empathy, the Leadership Attributes Study revealed participant's responses encompassed several key concepts.[6] These were:

- listen (to feel)
- care
- self-worth.

Such feeling and 'listening to the stories of others' (Participants 6 and 7) will encourage honest dialogue between people and 'help to open up people, not close them up.' (Participant 6) This will lead to a growth in authenticity within people themselves and the whole community.

Several participants spoke of moral community or a good community in terms of reaching out beyond oneself 'helping each individual reach their own soul/faith journey.' (Participant 2)

> Becoming other person-centred, where every person within that community should have a sense of belonging and being accepted. Being cared for and moving towards those values (of a community). (Participant 7)

This objective can be achieved through empathetic listening to each other and responding to people's needs. A moral community needs to be supported and nurtured by leaders who look, listen and feel. A leader should be able to respond spontaneously as the need arises. For example:

> Upon seeing me the first time since my mother's death he gave me a huge hug. In all my years, I have never been hugged so by another man – he was genuine in his feelings. This is an example of compassion and it is one I often use to describe what leadership practices/community building is about. (Participant 10)[7]

The leadership actions as described above help to develop self-worth and provide a sense of purpose for all members of a community, organisation and family. A leader 'realises how important a sense of self-worth is as it develops commitment to each other.' (Participant 4)

Participants spoke of the importance of a leader's display of respect for every person in every situation. However, as one participant felt, 'it is not always easy when people are coming from different perspectives.' (Participant 7)

A woman that sought to understand empathetically and then engage people in open dialogue was Edith Cowan. She strived to bring about change and growth in a diverse community so that it grew towards a more humane society. Born in Western Australia, Edith Cowan was a social justice advocate for women and children, magistrate, politician, philanthropist, wife and mother at the turn of the twentieth century.[8] She was alive to celebrate the Federation of Australia in 1901. Edith Cowan University of Western Australia is named after her.

A Woman of Grace – Edith Cowan

Edith Cowan was Australia's first woman parliamentarian and one of the first woman magistrates in the Children's Court. She introduced the Women's Legal Status Bill (enacted in Western Australia in 1923), which removed the ban on women practising law and other professions. Indeed, this can be heralded as one of the first Acts around the world that introduced the status of women as equal to that of a man in a professional and legal sense.

At the age of 59, Edith stood as the Nationalist Party candidate for the Legislative Assembly seat of West Perth. She only decided to run for office just four weeks before the election, as she thought not enough was being done about the rights of children and women. She defeated the sitting member, T. P. Draper, the Attorney-General, by 46 votes. In a bizarre twist of fate, he had been responsible for the Bill allowing women to stand for Parliament.

In her first speech in Parliament, Edith outlined what could be done to help children, women, wage earners and pensioners. Here is a little of what she said:

> I stand here today in the unique position of being the first woman in an Australian Parliament. I know many people think perhaps that it was not the wisest thing to do to send a woman into Parliament, and perhaps I should remind honourable members that one of the reasons why women and men also considered it advisable to do so, was because it was felt that men need a reminder sometimes from women beside them that will make them realise all that can be done for the race and for the home. I have been sent here more from that standpoint than from any other ... The views of both sides are more than ever needed in Parliament today. If men and women can work for the State side by side and represent all the different sections of the community, and if the male members of the house would be satisfied to allow women to help them and would accept their suggestions when they are offered,

> I cannot doubt that we should do very much better work in the community than was ever done before (From Cowan, E, debut speech in the House of Assembly [WA], 21 July 1921, Hansard, pp. 15-19).

Edith had some immediate success after winning the seat. When she complained that mothers taking prams on suburban trains had to pay a 'pram fare', the Minister for Railways replied that he would withdraw the charge at once.

Edith did not support the war (WWI), as she did not see it as a solution to international problems. But, as the war progressed, Edith saw that there were practical things to be done for the ordinary people involved. She was empathetic and compassionate towards those directly affected by the war. Western Australia was the first port of call in Australia for hospital ships coming back from the battlefields. Edith, without hesitation, helped organise welcoming committees for the personnel on the ships. She also established a Soldiers' Institute to provide soldiers with meals, rest and recreation. She was awarded an OBE for her work.

Edith was also credited with being a prominent activist for social justice. Below is a list of some of those groups of which she was a founder and/or a president or vice president:

- The Karrakatta Club (the Karrakatta Club became involved in the campaign for women's suffrage, successfully gaining the vote for women in 1899).
- House of Mercy (a home for unmarried mothers).
- The Women's Service Guild (the Guild lobbied for the building of Perth's King Edward Memorial Hospital for Women).
- Western Australia's National Council of Women.
- The Children's Protection Society (the Society had a major role in the introduction of children's courts).
- Foundation member of Co-Freemasonry in Western Australia.
- Red Cross Appeal Committee during WWI.
- Australian delegate to the 1925 International Conference of Women held in the United States.
- Royal Western Australian Historical Society.
- Planning of Western Australia's Centenary celebrations.

So what was it that drove this incredible woman towards such creditable ventures of virtue and strength touched by the gentleness of empathy? For Edith, it was her early childhood life. Her experiences gave insight to an amazing view of equality and the ability to empathetically and tactfully get her message across.

Sadly, her mother died in childbirth when Edith was seven years old and she was sent to boarding school. There she learnt the value of education for all people. Her father remarried and then murdered his second wife. He was tried and consequently hanged. Edith was fifteen years old.

She strived to achieve a better life and future for all children, women, the poor and those in need. Edith did this through her relentless passion for her own self-education, which she was prepared to share with everyone who would listen. The depth of Edith's personal pain brought out the best in her. Edith achieved a quiet grace that fuelled her empathetic ways of dealing with the suffering and pain of others.

So remember to use the gift of a loving silence when listening to the needs of others, and be willing to accept the empathy of others as they listen to you.

> Empathy is compassion and passion blending
> continuously within each one of us.
>
> ~Vicky McGahey~

> **Attribute in Reflective Action**
> **EMPATHY**
>
> *How can we build empathy into our daily lives?*
> **Simply ...**
> Do not intentionally seek to hurt anyone
> **Also**
> Do your best to listen with passion and compassion
> **And**
> Feel the needs of others
> **Then**
> Always be there

After significant analysis of the attributes, the following satellite attributes were found to be directly related to the key Leadership Attribute of *Empathy*:

- Compassion
- Passion.

The attributes of *Compassion* and *Passion* are the feeling attributes that will bring love into a world that is in need.

Compassion

> Never see a need without doing something about it.
> **Mary MacKillop**

> Compassion will cure more sins then condemnation.
> **Henry Ward Beecher**

Motto – listen to feel

Symbol – heart

Compassion means to be caring and patient. Compassion and courage go hand in hand. It takes great courage to be compassionate. Compassion requires trust in oneself, one's own intuitive judgment and wisdom. The action of compassion requires one to stop! And to listen! To shut out the endless chatter in your head! Stop and listen … listen … listen.

As Stephen Covey has often stated: Seek first to understand and then be understood.[9]

The word compassion has another word within it – passion. You literally and metaphorically cannot have com*passion* without *passion*.

Compassion reveals the feelings of passion; passion frees one to be compassionate.

A leader needs a compassionate and passionate heart with a quiet strength that is reassuringly persistent.

As you reflect upon the attribute of compassion, consider the following questions and jot down your thoughts. In doing so, you are engaging in a practice that will enrich your personal empathy (compassion).

1. Why does the world need compassion?
2. Why is compassion an important attribute for one to develop within themself? As a leader?
3. What is the simplest, most effective act of compassion? Give examples/stories.

4. Think of a place and time when you showed compassion? Was there an element of passion? Notice passion within the word compassion.
5. When has another person shown compassion to you?
6. How do you show compassion to those who have hurt others?
7. How do we balance compassion for the individual and compassion for the community or organisation? Environment? Give examples/stories.
8. What other thoughts do you have about compassion and passion? Do you agree there is a connection between the two?

The friendship between Mary MacKillop and Father Julian Tenison Woods is well documented.[10]

A Woman of Compassion – Saint Mary MacKillop

Mary MacKillop, Australia's first and only saint, displayed the gracious attribute of compassion. She was 37 years old when Gandhi was born and – with Father Julian Tenison Woods – had already established the first Australian order of Catholic nuns, the Sisters of St Joseph of the Sacred Heart. Mary was passionate about life and the order she founded. There are many stories of Mary displaying fortitude, compassion and forgiveness while always maintaining a graceful heart of love and a burning desire for reconciliation.

There were many disappointments for Mary, such as excommunication, betrayal by those close to her, unkind and untruthful words and losing her position as Mother-General of the order only to be reinstated several years later.

But there were also many great joys, such as the school that she and Father Woods built together, the first years of the formation of the Congregation of the Sisters of St Joseph, the time spent in Rome and Scotland and the resounding achievement of the rule and constitution for the order as a 'stand alone' institute, granted by the Pope. This meant that the Sisters could operate without the interference of the local bishops.

There are many, many letters written by Mary that are filled with love, passion and happiness of a life well lived in the service of others.

Together, Father Woods and Mary diligently wrote the rule and constitution for the new religious order for Rome's approval (The Holy See). But, through the interference of several Australian bishops, it was changed. Mary agreed to the changes much to the disappointment of Father Julian. This caused much ill-feeling and resentment in Father Julian. He refused to have anything to do with Mary or the Sisters for some 15 years before his death. Mary's desire for reconciliation and her willingness to forgive was clearly displayed in her relentless efforts to be reunited with Father Woods. She kept writing to him on special occasions and birthdays, and would not hear or say an unkind word about the co-founder.

Ultimately, her persistence and goodwill were rewarded. Shortly before his death, Father Woods agreed to meet with Mary. However, the first time she visited, the people looking after him took offence to her visit and the door was shut in her face. Father Woods wrote a letter to apologise and soon she was able to visit him. Mary visited him many times before he died. Though little is known of what she shared with Father Woods, one can only imagine the joy and peace they both found in reliving happy times, the current achievements of the Sisters and of the possible future for the order they had founded together.

Mary MacKillop had her own catchphrase and war cry 'never see a need without doing something about it.' Indeed, she led a life with a graceful vision for a grace-filled mission that was a call to action in the service of others.

In the Leadership Attributes study, a participant made an intuitive statement:[11]

> The interesting thing about compassion is that it is far easier to destroy an enemy than be compassionate towards them. (Participant 10)

It was Abraham Lincoln who said, 'The best way to destroy an enemy is by making him your friend.'

One of Life's More Memorable Experiences – Vicky McGahey

A few years ago, I spent some time in a jungle with a good friend of mine. We were part of a larger group. It was one of the most valuable experiences of my life ... not so much the jungle, but the time I spent with my companion. I learnt what it was to be passionate about life and the experiences it dishes out. Most importantly, I learnt that I had the capacity to truly empathise and show compassion. I made my own desires and goals for the adventure mirror my companion's goals. Below is a brief description of what transpired over the endless hours of walking up and down the hills of an extensive jungle mountain range. This was part of a speech I gave to the local Returned and Services League (RSL) and to my own Rotary Club:

The story begins...

I want you to imagine you are in a tropical jungle – jungle here, jungle there, jungle everywhere – on an island not too far from Australia.

You are walking along a well-worn track going up hill and down hill – up and down, with no flat stretches at all. You have been doing this for four days. The days comprise 12-14 hours of walking and talking.

Your guides are two local people who assist you and your Australian friend. Along the way, at a crossroad, you meet a local teacher who decides to tag along.

Your Australian companion is a lady of some years – considering the nature of the track she is walking – but her resilience is phenomenal. Her sense of purpose and resolve is unwavering. There is no pain she cannot overcome and conquer ... and you know this!

You are part of a larger group (12 other Australians). They have had six-hour walking days (not 12) but to the joy of you and your companion, there is always great glee as you walk into the camp and the site is well prepared for your late-night arrival.

So the long days in a relentless and endless, hot, sticky jungle are not really all that hard. You spend the hours talking and singing songs that range from 'My teacher had an apple with a green worm inside' to grand operettas and a resounding version of the 'Hallelujah Chorus'. Even the jungle birds join in and, to your surprise, your teacher companion knows the 'Hallelujah Chorus' quite well – he was taught by missionaries who have long since gone.

On this particular evening, you and your companions have descended a steep hillside to face yet another challenge – a bamboo bridge that stretches some ten or so metres across a ravine with raging rapids below.

It is now pitch black! Even moonlight cannot penetrate the solid walls of jungle that stretch relentlessly around you so you take out your head torches to discover that only two of them work ... and one of those is beginning to fade. Verbal communication is not possible for there is a frightening and deafening roaring sound all around you. But you know where it is coming from ... it is the raging, rapid-filled waters and waterfall below the bamboo bridge that you are about to cross. So communication is hand signals under the dimly lit torches.

Your local guides seem worried ... very worried. From their signals, you get the feeling that the bridge should have been bigger, with a rail to hold as you crossed. Obviously, this was lost to the deafening raging rapids below.

Two at a time, you cross the rickety bridge. Your companion first with a guide holding her hand as he walks backwards over the bridge. The local teacher follows close behind them to ensure no-one falls. Through the darkness you can just see that they have made it to the other side. So you and the remaining guide commence your crossing.

The first step is OK! On the second and third steps, you smile at the guide facing you – holding your hand and walking backwards. You use your free arm to balance. By now you are halfway across and the bamboo is sagging under your feet as you sense a jerky movement. Then, even above the raging sounds of rapids below, comes the sound you will never forget! 'CRACK! CRACK!' It is the sound of bamboo giving way under your feet.

As you look down with the head-torch light on but very dim, by now you see the jungle twine in tatters and the bamboo sticks shaking, sagging and cracking beneath your feet.

Instinctively, you look into the eyes of your guide and yell 'run'. He turns and immediately begins to run. You look at the back of his head and take off close behind him.

Leadership Attributes for Women and Men

You make it to the other side - but only just - as the bridge was in tatters and about to collapse. Needless to say, your companion was pleased and relieved, as she'd heard the cracking sound through the darkness and thought the worst.

You are taking this journey to get to a sacred memorial site - a memorial to the young men who fought and died along the very track you walk. The memorial is Isurava! The island is New Guinea! The track is Kokoda!

The memorial consists of four black marble pillars in a semi-circle. Each pillar is engraved with a virtue: *Courage, Endurance, Mateship* and *Sacrifice*. The pillars stand as a testament to the valour and courage of those who fought and died during the Kokoda campaign.

It is amazing how the experiences of Kokoda can set the sail for change, growth and discovery. On the track, I was prepared to walk at a slower pace in order to spend time with a person who became more and more of a friend with each step we took along that relentless track. It did not seem like compassionate service at the time, but indeed it was. I received more from that experience than I put in. The gift of a little of my time was worthwhile. My companion's insights into life and a topic of growing interest to me (politics) along with her good humour, laughter and love have been a continuous flow of passion, compassion and power that has led me to seek to serve. My companion will remain forever close to my heart.

And is that not the truth? We always get more back from the giving of compassionate service than we put in. And, as the Dalai Lama reminds us:

> Love and compassion are necessities, not luxuries.
> Without them humanity cannot survive.
> **Dalai Lama**

As a final word:
> Compassion and courage go hand-in-hand.
> It takes great courage to be compassionate.
> **~Vicky McGahey~**

Attribute in Reflective Action
COMPASSION

How can we build compassion into our daily lives?

Simply ...

Care

Also

Listen, so as to feel compassion

And

Become passionate about compassion

Then

Be compassionate

The next satellite attribute for *Empathy* is *Passion*.

Passion

> The people who get on in this world are
> the people who get up and look for the
> circumstances they want, and if they
> can't find them, make them.
>
> **George Bernard Shaw**

> I'd rather be a failure at something I love
> than a success at something I hate.
>
> **George Burns**

Motto – listen to feel

Symbol – heart

Passion is enthusiasm and persistence that flows from the heart. A leader can use this attribute to motivate people towards actions that will create and sustain a sense of community and a sense of belonging. Empathy and passion are catalysts for creating a sense of belonging for all people.

The need for leaders to be close to and passionate about nature is mirrored in religions and particularly in Eastern teachings. For example, Buddhism and the *Tao Te Ching* written by Lao Tzu (Taoism) have many references to leaders, passion, the heart and nature.

> Tao leaders live close to nature.
> Their actions flow from the heart.
> In words they are true;
> In decisions, just. (Tao, 8)
>
> **(Dreher, 1997)**[12]

A leader can use this attribute to motivate others towards actions that will create and sustain a sense of community – a sense of belonging. In this way, a leader can effectively create an environment where authentic and trusting relationships thrive.

As you reflect upon the attribute of passion, consider the following questions, and jot down your thoughts. In doing so, you are engaging in a practice that will enrich your personal empathy (passion).

1. Why is passion considered an attribute?
2. Why is passion an important attribute to develop within oneself? For leaders and leadership?
3. What are you most passionate about? Name it. Give examples/stories. Hint: to help with the answer to this question ...
   - What makes you happiest in your life? What excites you?
   - What do people thank you for?
   - When was the last time you were in state of flow? In other words, you totally lost track of time? What were you doing?
   - If you won a large sum of money, three months after winning it, what would you be doing?
4. Who do you look up to? Who inspires you? Why? Give examples/stories.

In his book *Mastery*, Robert Greene describes Charles Darwin's passion for discovering how life is continuing to evolve.[13] The following story is based on Greene's version and another insightful text.[14]

Collections - Charles Darwin

Charles Darwin knew what he wanted to do from an early age. He just did not know how that need could translate into a job and income.

Darwin never thought much of his own intellect. He once said of himself, 'my power to follow a long and purely abstract train of thought is very limited.'

But he had one extraordinary attribute. Darwin had passion and was passionate about his work. As a child, he had an overriding passion - collecting biological specimens. Darwin would spend hours wandering the local fields, roads and byways collecting specimens. He would bring them home and meticulously mount them.

His father was a doctor who wanted Charles to follow in his footsteps. He enrolled him at the University of Edinburgh but, unfortunately, Darwin did not do very well in the subject. His father next tried to secure him a career in the church. As Darwin was preparing for this, a former professor told him that the ship HMS *Beagle* was to leave port to sail around the world. The ship needed a biologist to accompany the crew in order to collect specimens that would be sent back to England. Needless to say, Darwin took the job and the rest is history.

The voyage was a perfect outlet for Darwin's passion. He collected an amazing array of insect specimens, as well as fossils and bones. His passion grew as he studied and collected specimens that displayed the variety of life on Earth. Through this passion, he began to question the origins of species.

Darwin was able to pour most of his energy into his passion. After five years at sea, he returned to England and devoted the rest of his life to the single task of formulating his theory of evolution.

To be a leader, to inspire others to follow, you need to be passionate and display that passion. It is from passion that you become alive with energy and focus. People will see this and want to be part of it. You don't need to have extraordinary talent or intellect or brilliance to have passion. Passion can come from a deep and powerful yearning to know and understand a particular subject, object or abstract truth. It is this yearning that is often a true reflection of the self and a person's uniqueness.

The reality is that we often equate thinking and intellectual ability with success and achievement. Some would equate such reasoning to becoming a successful leader. However, it is the emotional aspect of being human that allows us to truly become masters of a field of study rather than just participants. This is also true of leadership. To become a leader you need to be a master or at least be on the journey to being one.

Being passionate is raw emotion exposed. This can frighten us. But it is what motivates and energises us so that we can overcome almost anything. It is what creates followership (followers) and sustains (ensures) their continued support.

All the great masters of the world displayed the attribute of passion in abundance. These include Leonardo da Vinci, Benjamin Franklin, Wolfgang Amadeus Mozart, Johann Wolfgang von Goethe, the poet John Keats, the scientist Michael Faraday, Thomas Edison, Albert Einstein, Henry Ford, the jazz artist John Coltrane and, of course, Charles Darwin.

The Leadership Attributes Study revealed several key points about passion:[15]

> Passion with persistence is a feel-good thing. It is fundamentally a moral attribute. (Participant 8)

> Passion should not be confused with enthusiasm. For example, the following description of a moral leader: 'now he was passionate about the things he thought were important but he was never enthusiastic. He would just quietly work through them.' (Participant 4)

And:

> People with fire in the belly – passion. The real challenge is to be able to continue and work with that passion even when things get tough. I like the persistence that comes with the passion. (Participant 3)

However, a community must be able to discuss openly that which is considered good and bad within the community, for, as one participant stated:

> A leader has to have persistence and enthusiasm that flows from the heart, but that may not be moral. What is in my heart may not be what is true and good. (Participant 7)

Several participants cited examples such as Adolf Hitler as leaders with passion but questionable principles, beliefs and values.

> Passion implies almost unwavering commitment – a zeal – enthusiasm to the highest level. It comes from the heart … with a sort of unwavering sense of commitment. (Participant 2)

For many of us, our job is just a job. It helps us to make money so as we can live and get by day to day. There are many stories of people who throughout the ages have held down a job to make ends meet and then during their free time actually worked on things that they were passionate about.

The Dalai Lama is adamant that we must strive to achieve happiness in all we do.[16] It is a happy person who can make their passion and passionate work into their job. One such person to achieve this was Antonie van Leeuwenhoek (the father of microscopy).[17]

The Microscopic World – Antonie van Leeuwenhoek

Antonie van Leeuwenhoek was born in 1632 in the Netherlands and, at the age of 16, he was apprenticed to a linen draper in Delft. Here, van Leeuwenhoek grew fascinated with the lenses used to inspect the cloth. As a dashing young 22-year-old, he married and opened a draper's shop, where he sold cloth, needles and ribbons to support himself and his family. Still, his fascination with lenses remained, along with the microscopic world he was discovering daily. Van Leeuwenhoek's real passion was science.

In his spare time, van Leeuwenhoek would make magnifying glasses, which he used to build microscopes. Over a number of years, he made 247 microscopes and used them to examine drinking water, rainwater and just about anything else he could. Through his work, van Leeuwenhoek discovered strange microorganisms, protozoa and bacteria. In 1673, he wrote to the Royal Society of London and described his findings. The members of the society were amazed that a person without any formal education had made such an important contribution to science. Van Leeuwenhoek continued to write and publish his work while still running his shop. Eventually the Royal Society made him a member and, in later years, he became world famous.

Antonie van Leeuwenhoek had great passion for his work. Upon his death, he bequeathed his lens and microscopes to the Society for future research. His life-changing work continues to revolutionise our world today.

As Julia Pitt – a trained success coach who works with people to establish their goals and achieve their aspirations – stated in her article: 'A life without passion is no life at all.'[18]

> Passion with persistence is enthusiasm that
> flows from the heart and soul.
> ~Vicky McGahey~

> **Attribute in Reflective Action**
> **PASSION**
>
> *How can we build passion into our daily lives?*
> **Simply ...**
> Stop ... listen ... to what lies within
> **Also**
> Seek the passion within others
> **And**
> Love the object of your passion
> **Then**
> Be the passion

As previously mentioned, empathy is compassion and passion growing and flowing within us. A leader should always be passionate towards seeking the truth by being enthusiastic about that which they feel is good and true. In other words, the leader should use their intuition and feel for the truth. Hence the need for the fourth key Leadership Attribute of *Intuition*.

Chapter 7

INTUITION

with the satellite attribute of **Risk**

The intuitive mind is a sacred gift and the rational mind is a faithful servant. We have created a society that honours the servant and has forgotten the gift.

Albert Einstein

The intellect has little to do on the road to discovery. There comes a leap in consciousness, call it intuition or what you will, the solution comes to you and you don't know how or why.

Albert Einstein

Motto – the perception of truth

Symbol – soul and rainbow

Intuition

Intuition is said to be an unconscious form of knowledge that rests just below the conscious level of thought. It is an inner voice.

The inner voice or human intuition has long been regarded as one of the best tools for finding solutions to questions of purpose (life, personal and community direction). The use of intuition can be applied to the arts and sciences or any field in which there are complex elements.

The Leadership Attribute of *Risk* is the satellite attribute of *Intuition*. It is discussed within this chapter.

Intuition is a sense of knowing something without evidence. It is about the realisation that sometimes things are not as they seem. Intuition comes from within; it's a deep sense of knowing without knowing why.

Some people are more naturally attuned to using their intuition in both extreme and everyday circumstances without even realising it. However, consciously using your intuition gives you an edge over your circumstances. Intuition can save money, make money, save your life or the lives of loved ones. It can save you from hiring the wrong person or taking the wrong job. Here is a story about a real-life situation:

The Voice Within - Vicky McGahey

How often do you hear people say, 'I think I have made the right decision,' instead of saying, 'I know I have made the right decision'? I could cite several examples, but the one I mostly reflect upon happened many years ago.

I remember as a small child I attended a family wedding. The bride, my cousin, was about to walk down the aisle. She turned to her father and said, 'I cannot do this!'

Her father held her and replied, 'It's just nerves.'

She kept saying 'I cannot do this!' several times and began to cry – not for happiness I feared.

Two beautiful sons and 11 years later, she was divorced and much happier.

Leadership Attributes for Women and Men

The truth is, we often ignore the voice of intuition for far too long. Intuition is easily swept aside because we believe being intuitive is nothing special, but ignoring it is a mistake. This thinking can lead to a waste of a natural ability that almost everyone will admit exists though few feel they can use it on a regular basis for their own well-being. Intuition is very closely tied to who we are. It is linked to our principles, values, beliefs and practices.

Leadership is a complex concept that, at times, requires fast decision-making and instant action. The more attuned we are to our own principles, values, beliefs and practices, the more effective we are as a leader.

There are many stories of people using their creative, imaginative and intuitive powers to create new possibilities and inventions. Here are a few:

- Einstein: It is said he had a 'black room' in his house, where no light could enter. It was a place where he would empty his mind.
- Descartes, the father of rational thinking: It is said his theory came to him in a dream.
- Ada Lovelace: The prophet of the computer age was very creative and used her imagination to express the potential for computers in 1843.
- Benjamin Franklin: He was well known for his ability to create instruments to assist him in his work. He invented bifocals and the mechanical arm.
- Mozart: Famously, he once said of his compositions, 'whence and how do they come? I do not know, and I have nothing to do with it.'
- Isaac Newton: When an apple fell on his head, the event captured his imagination and the theory of gravity was born.
- Archimedes: When the king suspected that his new crown was not made of solid gold, he asked Archimedes to prove this. On contemplating the problem, this famous Greek scientist and mathematician had a 'Eureka' moment in a bath.

Intuition

Einstein, Plato, Jung, Franklin, Michelangelo and Gandhi all spoke of intuition as the most important aspect of an individual's thinking. All used their intuition to help inspire them to make many significant contributions to benefit humankind.

Einstein once stated: 'I believe in intuition and inspiration ... at times I feel certain I am right while not knowing the reason.'[1]

And, as others citing Einstein have stated:

> Imagination is more important than knowledge. For knowledge is limited, whereas imagination embraces the entire world, stimulating progress, giving birth to evolution.[2]

The work of people like Schön (1984) on reflective practice has legitimised the use of intuition and sensing in organisational decision-making.[3] The five senses are sight, sound, taste, touch and smell. The sixth 'sense' is intuition – the feeling within or gut response. Schön believes in reflection in action that allows for instant critique and intuitive understanding of experience.

As you reflect upon the attribute of intuition, review the following questions and jot down your thoughts. In doing so, you are engaging in a practice that will enrich your personal intuition.

1. Why should we use our intuition?
2. Why is intuition an important attribute for one to develop within themself? As a leader?
3. How can I tell my intuition apart from my agenda? How do I know when I am perceiving something or when I just think something because I want it to be that way? Give examples/stories.
4. When was the last time you used your intuition in making a decision?
5. What can you do to allow intuitive thought to have a greater role in your vision and mission planning?

When in a situation requiring intuition try the following direct questions. Give it a go now! Think of a situation! First! Name the situation! Write it down!

- 'What is really going on with ____?' Keep asking this question and writing down the answer. Keep at it and go deeper into all possibilities … chances are that is what is going on! Then,
- 'What do I need to know about ____?'
- 'Why do I feel stuck/confused/blocked?'
- 'How can I improve this situation?'
- 'What is the best course of action to take regarding ____?'
- 'Is there something that I am missing or not seeing? If so, what is it?'[4]

Benjamin Franklin was a person who mastered his inner gift of intuition. The following story is adapted from Robert Greene's book, *Mastery*.[5]

Intuitive Creations – Benjamin Franklin

There are many stories about Benjamin Franklin's natural ability to dream up ideas and then create practical objects that really made a difference in his life and the lives of others.

In his 70s and 80s, Franklin was still coming up with advanced ideas on health and medicine, weather, physics, geophysics, evolution, the use of aircraft for military and commercial purposes, and more. As he aged, he applied his inventiveness to helping himself and others. He invented bifocals to improve eyesight; the mechanical 'long arm', a device that enabled him to reach books high up on a bookshelf; and the rolling press, so that he could make copies of his work quickly and efficiently in the comfort of his own home.

In the final years of Franklin's life he became known as a great philosopher. His thoughts and insights into politics and the future of America astounded many at the time. Some believed he had magical abilities. William Pierce, a delegate to the Constitutional Convention, met Franklin near the end of his life and wrote:

> Dr Franklin is well known to be the greatest philosopher of the present age; all the operations of nature he seems to understand … He is 82 years old, and possesses an activity of mind equal to a youth of 25 years of age.

Actually, these abilities were Franklin's inherent and profound mastery of his own intuition, which he had developed over the years. He was a master at using his inner knowing to guide him in the creation of his many diverse works.

Another such person is Ada Lovelace. She is known as 'the prophet of the computer age.'[6]

The Prophet of the Computer Age - Ada Lovelace

The daughter of famed poet Lord Byron, Augusta Ada Byron, Countess of Lovelace - known as Ada Lovelace - was born on 10 December 1815 in London. Her mother wisely insisted that Ada be tutored in mathematics, not just the humanities, as was the tradition for girls at the time. A gifted mathematician from an early age, Ada wrote the instructions for the first computer program in the mid-1800s, and she is considered the first computer programmer.

When she was 17 years of age, Ada fortuitously met Charles Babbage, known as 'the father of the computer', at a party where he demonstrated the working of his difference engine. This machine was designed to perform mathematical calculations. She was intrigued and fascinated by Babbage's ideas. He was amazed at her insight into the workings and possible future uses of the engine. The meeting began a mentoring relationship where Babbage ensured Ada received the best tutorage by studying advanced mathematics with University of London professor Augustus de Morgan.

Italian engineer Luigi Federico Menabrea wrote an article in French on Babbage's analytical engine - a subsequent project to the difference engine. Ada was asked to translate the article into English. While doing this, she made extensive notes of her own thoughts and ideas about the use of the machine. Indeed, her notes were three times longer than the article. Her work was published in 1843, in an English science journal.

Ada described the notion of coding using symbols, letters and numbers. She also discussed how the engine could repeat a set of instructions over and over - in today's computing world, this process is known as looping. Ada believed it could create music or graphics if given the right input data. She once wrote, 'The Analytical Engine weaves algebraic patterns just as the Jacquard loom weaves flowers and leaves.'

Ada's article attracted little attention when she was alive. In her later years, she tried to develop mathematical schemes for winning at gambling. Unfortunately, her schemes failed and put her in financial peril. She overcame this obsession. Ada died on 27 November 1852.

Ada Lovelace's contributions to the field of computer science remained unknown until 1953 when B. V. Bowden republished her notes in his article, 'Faster Than Thought: A Symposium on Digital Computing Machines.'

Since then, Ada has received many posthumous honours for her work, including a society that has established an International Day for the celebration of women's contributions to science and technology (2nd Tuesday in October). In 1980, the U.S. Department of Defense named a newly developed computer language 'Ada', after Lovelace.

Ada intuitively saw beyond the analytical face value of the engine and dreamed of great opportunities. She cast a light into the future of the coming computer age and caught a glimpse of the possibilities – just as Michelangelo, Galileo and many other creative thinkers of our time have done.

In his book titled *Mastery*, Robert Greene speculated what depth of understanding such mastery could have reached if people like Benjamin Franklin and others had lived longer.[7] Perhaps in the future, with life expectancy increasing, we will witness more people like Benjamin Franklin, in the later years of their life, creating a better, brighter and more prosperous future for our world.

Many of the participants in the Leadership Attributes Study reflected upon the intuitive and the spiritual nature of leadership, which enabled each leader to gain insight into themselves.[8]

Leaders should strive to develop the 'ability to manage what I call the symbolic dimension of leadership – having a sense of inwardness is important.' (Participant 4); the 'ability to reflect – consider oneself.'

(Participants 2 and 9); and a good 'sense of understanding of themselves as people and not an individual sense but as a humanitarian sense. It is a double-sided coin.' (Participant 6)

The participants' responses surrounded several key concepts. These were:

- know thyself
- insight
- reflection.

One participant spoke quite poignantly:

(Leaders) make explicit that which is implicit. This is one of the big challenges for our leaders today. People do not like the degree of ambiguity that goes with this. They don't have the personal spiritual development that goes with it. They see it as an unnecessary function – give me a formula, give me that – they have missed the point. (Participant 9)

Other participants said: 'The need for "connection" is a powerful motivator' (Participant 4); 'Intuition is having a sense of connection' (Participants 2 and 7); and 'It means being able to keep that [attribute of intuition] at the forefront of your thinking all the time.' (Participant 2)

One participant linked intuition to the spiritual realm: 'So it is a state of grace – a continual state of grace. I had not thought of it in those terms, but that is what it is.' (Participant 2)

As mentioned earlier, in recent times, researchers and leaders have looked upon leadership as a venture into the soul – into oneself.[9] Wenniger (1997), a researcher on women's issues and moral reasoning, describes this venture as a discovery of self and the giving of gifts, such as the gifts of love, the gifts of authorship (freeing the intelligence) and the gifts of significance (celebration of rituals, stories and ceremonies). Wenniger speaks of the soul in relation to community spirit:

Leading with soul is dangerous business. It takes courage to accept our imperfections and be vulnerable. You need to be authentic to bring your essential self into your working relationships, but that's what it takes to nurture community spirit.[10]

History is full of leaders who took intuition to a spiritual level and a state of grace. Examples of leaders who inspired through their religious beliefs and personal ideology are Mahatma Gandhi, Mother Teresa and Mary MacKillop. They believed that the journey was more important than the destination or the end point. They would say, 'one should leave the final outcome and destination in God's control.'

Set your sights, follow your vision but know that the final destination is not in your control. The wonderful story of the ugly duckling is a perfect example of this concept. The original story was written by the ultimate storyteller Hans Christian Andersen.[11] Are there many people who have not heard this story? I fear that too many of today's schoolchildren have not. The following version is my adaptation of the original story.

The Ugly Duckling

This is the story of a little bird that suffers abuse from those around him just because he does not look the same and, therefore, does not fit in.

It is a beautiful summer day. The sun shines warmly on an old house near a river. Behind the house, a mother duck is sitting on four eggs. 'Tchick.' One by one, the eggs begin to break open. Out tumbled three tiny ducklings as yellow as butter and as soft as down.

'What a beautiful little family I have,' thought the mother duck.

She looked down and saw that one egg - the biggest egg of all - had not yet hatched. Mother duck sits and sits on the big egg. At last, it breaks open, 'Tchick, tchick!' Out jumps the last baby duckling. It looks big and strong. It is white, fuzzy and ugly to look at ... at least from a duck's point of view.

The next day, mother duck takes all her little ducklings to the river. She jumps into the water and the baby ducklings follow. They all swim and play together. The ugly duckling swims better than all the other ducklings.

'Quack, quack! Come with me to the farmyard!' says mother duck to her baby ducklings and they all follow her there.

The farmyard is very noisy. The poor ugly duckling is so unhappy there. The hens peck him, the rooster flies at him and the other ducks bite him.

One evening, just as the sun sets, there came a large flock of beautiful birds out of the bushes. The duckling had never seen birds like them before. They were swans, and they curved their graceful necks, while their soft plumage shone with dazzling whiteness. They uttered a singular cry as they spread their glorious wings and flew away from those cold regions to warmer countries across the sea. As they rose higher and higher in the air, the ugly little duckling felt quite a strange sensation as he watched them. He whirled himself in the water like a wheel, stretched out his neck towards them, and uttered a cry so strange that he frightened himself! Could he ever forget those beautiful, happy birds? When at last they were out of sight, he dived under the water, and rose again, almost beside himself with excitement. He knew not the names of these birds, nor where they had flown, but he felt towards them as he had never felt for any other bird in the world. He was not envious of these beautiful creatures, but wished to be as lovely as they.

Soon, it is winter and everything is white with snow. The river is covered with ice and the ugly duckling is cold and unhappy. Then comes the spring and the sun shines warm upon him. Everything is fresh and green.

One morning, the ugly duckling sees the beautiful swans again. He knows them. He wants so much to swim with them in the river, but he is afraid of them. So he runs to the river and he looks into the water. There, reflected in the water, he sees a beautiful swan.

'Is that me?' he wonders. 'Wait! It is me!'

He is no longer an ugly duckling. He is a beautiful white swan.

'Why did I not listen to what my heart was saying to me?' he cried. 'I knew I was a beautiful swan underneath it all. I just needed time to grow!'

The other swans approach him and welcome him. He was at home at last.

He had been led to believe that he was different! And he could see he was different! Yet he instinctively knew there was a place for him as he felt an affinity with the migrating swans. He held onto this hope throughout a chilly winter. In fact, that hope kept him alive until he once again heard and saw the swans. Then, by looking at his own reflection in the water, he realised he was indeed a beautiful swan.

The story of the ugly duckling has many messages. One is the need to accept differences — diversity is another Leadership Attribute.

Being guided by your intuition will take considerable courage. It requires us to accept change and challenge the preconceived ideas of others and ourselves. Therefore:

> Be guided by your intuition for it is the
> direct perception of truth.
>
> ~Vicky McGahey[12]~

So:

> Stop! Take a look at yourself —
> a deep look at yourself and discover.
>
> ~Vicky McGahey~

> **Attribute in Reflective Action**
> **INTUITION**
>
> *How can we build intuition into our daily lives?*
> **Simply ...**
> Listen, feel and share
> **Also**
> Listen to the voice within – the answers to
> all questions lie within and not without
> **And**
> Be still and watch
> **Then**
> Know thyself and act in truth

After significant analysis of the Leadership Attributes, the satellite attribute of *Risk* was found to be directly related to the key Leadership Attribute of *Intuition*.

Make sure you always use your intuition when engaging in risk.

Risk

> Security is mostly a superstition. It does not exist in nature ... avoiding danger is no safer in the long run than outright exposure. Life is either a daring adventure or nothing at all.
>
> **Helen Keller,** *The Open Door*

> A ship is always safe at the shore – but that is NOT what it is built for.
>
> **Albert Einstein**

Motto – the perception of truth

Symbol – soul and rainbow

Fear of the outcome of an action is the reason why people fear to take risks. It was Gandhi who believed that we should not worry about the outcome of our actions when the action is in line with our principles and values. Gandhi used to say that we are not responsible for the outcome.[13] Our duty is to make sure that our motives are pure and our means are consistent with our beliefs. If we take care of our motives and means, the rest will follow naturally.

A leader needs to be willing to trust in themselves and others for risk taking to be done without fear.

As you reflect upon the attribute of risk, consider the following questions and jot down your thoughts. In doing so, you are engaging in a practice that will enrich your personal intuition (risk).

1. Why is risk taking an important attribute for one to develop within themself? As a leader?
2. Why take risks? What are the advantages? What are the disadvantages?
3. How willing are you to take risks? Why?
4. What are you afraid of? How is fear related to risk taking? Give examples/stories.
5. When you are unsure of the outcome when trying a new idea, how do you react? Give examples/stories.

6. When was the last time you took a risk? A personal risk? A leadership risk? Give examples/stories.
7. What is the worst-case story you can think of when taking a risk?
8. Think of a possible risk in the future?
   - What can you gain?
   - What can you lose?
   - What happens if you do not take the risk? If you do not change?
9. Have you ever shared in taking a risk with another?

Fear of success is very real and can be debilitating in so many ways. Too often we hide our true talents and abilities under a bushel.

Explorers are renowned for their risk taking. History speaks for itself, with names like Douglas Mawson, Burke and Wills, Lewis and Clark, Christopher Columbus and Captain James Cook. Without their willingness to accept the challenge and the consequences of their actions, humankind would not have had the wonderful role models and examples of what can be achieved. The nineteenth century is littered with aviators and deep-sea divers who took considerable risks (including risking their lives) to advance humankind. Every new-frontier pioneer took the risks in their stride. For:

> Living at risk is jumping off the cliff and
> building your wings on the way down.
>
> **Ray Bradbury**

We can visit YouTube documentaries and TED talks to see modern-day risk takers at work. One such person is Dr Sylvia Earle.[14]

Taking Risks - Dr Sylvia Earle

Sylvia Earle is an octogenarian oceanographer, marine biologist and author. She is a National Geographic explorer-in-residence. Sylvia catalogues and studies the ocean's inhabitants from a tiny submarine that takes her hundreds of metres under the sea. Sylvia has said of herself that she is a risk taker - 'no risk, no reward!'

Sylvia loves what she does and with so much more to discover and explore, she is not about to retire. It is the ocean that drives the way our world works. Sylvia sees herself as a child asking the why, who, what and how questions of life. She believes that as humans we are gifted with this amazing capacity to shape the world around us and to adapt it to suit our needs.

Sylvia's beliefs are supported in the biblical parable called 'The Parable of the Talents', which speaks of the gifts and talents we can use to shape our world.

The Parable of the Talents - Matthew 25: 14-30

Preparing for a journey, a man summoned his servants and entrusted his property to them, according to each man's ability; to the first he gave five talents (a sum of money), to another he gave two talents, and to another he gave one talent. Then he went away.

The servant who had received five talents went off at once, traded with them, and made five more talents. In the same way, the one who had been given two talents made two more. But the one who had received one talent went off and dug a hole in the ground and buried his master's money in it.

After a long time, the master of those servants came and settled accounts with them. The one who had received five talents came forward, bringing five more talents, saying, 'Master, you handed me five talents; see, I have made five more talents.'

His master said to him, 'Well done, good and trustworthy servant; you have been trustworthy in a few things, I will put you in charge of many things; enter into the joy of your master.'

And the one who had been given two talents also came forward, saying, 'Master, you handed over two talents to me; see, I have made two more talents.'

His master said to him, 'Well done, good and trustworthy servant; you have been trustworthy in a few things, I will put you in charge of many things; enter into the joy of your master.'

Then the one who had received one talent came forward, saying, 'Master, I knew that you were a harsh man, reaping where you did not sow, and gathering where you did not scatter seed; so I was afraid, and I went and buried your talent in the ground. Here you have what is yours.'

But his master replied, 'You wicked and lazy servant! You knew, did you, that I reap where I did not sow, where I did not scatter? Then you should have invested my money with the bankers, and on my return I would have received what was my own with interest.'

Turning to his servants the master demanded, 'Take the talent from him, and give it to the one with the ten talents. For to all those who have, more will be given, and they will have in abundance! But from those who have nothing, even what they have will be taken away. As for this worthless slave, throw him into the outer darkness, where there will be weeping and gnashing of teeth.'

The talents, as described in this story, do not represent only money and property, they represent natural talents and spiritual gifts.

From a Christian perspective, the Lord has entrusted us with many things: money, talents and gifts. He expects us to not just conserve these things but to grow them every day. This means taking risks, and not allowing the fear of failure and ridicule stop us from pursuing success. Without such boldness, Christianity would never have grown in Palestine; it never would have made it to Antioch, Greece, and Rome. The tenacity and faith of St Paul, St Peter, the Apostles and early Christians is well documented in history and celebrated in church tradition.

From a leadership perspective, it means having the courage to take bold initiatives as we lead sometimes from the front, sometimes from behind, but hopefully mainly from within the pack. In this way we grow, and the risks we take become less fearsome.

The Leadership Attributes Study revealed many interesting points about risk taking in leadership:[15]

> The willingness to take risks is the notion of having a strong commitment to something and not letting the fear of change stop you from being committed. (Participant 2)

The concept of risk can be easily associated with other leadership attributes. As one participant stated:

Being honest (integrity), then being guided by what you deeply believe (intuition), and then trying to tap into what others believe (judgment), being able to make a stand (prophecy) and that sometimes is risky business, but it is also trusting that it will be okay and work out alright. (Participant 8)

Another participant said: 'You have got to take risks and hope your intuition is right.' (Participant 1)

This brings to light an important point:

> Always use your intuition when taking a risk.
> **Vicky McGahey**

It is interesting to note that researchers at Vanderbilt University in Nashville and Albert Einstein College of Medicine in New York City found that people who take risks experience a rush of dopamine – a chemical in the body that makes us feel good every time we have a novel experience.

'We're not suggesting you become an adrenaline junkie,' said a researcher. 'You don't need a passport to have a sense of adventure. Instead, think about how to build your courage muscles.'[16]

There are many people in their 50s who put their career on hold to go back to school and university. Many people end unhappy long-term relationships, which has helped free up their energies for more positive pursuits. Here is a story of risk taking featuring Roz Savage.[17]

Risk Taking – Roz Savage

Several years ago, Roz Savage quit her high-powered London job to become an ocean rower. She's crossed the Atlantic, Pacific and Indian Oceans – all solo – the first for a woman.

The change in 'jobs' happened because she grew more and more uncomfortable with her life. She was getting older and wanted a challenge. One day, she sat down and began to write her obituary.

She wrote one for the life she was leading and another for the life she would have liked to have led. Roz realised that she needed to take action. She could not just sit back and expect happiness to find her. She needed to step out of her comfort zone and she found it quite uncomfortable. Roz spent the next few years exploring her options, making significant changes to her life through 'letting some things go.'

Through rowing and fundraising, Roz is helping to raise awareness of the shocking amount of global garbage - particularly plastics - in the oceans and how it affects marine life. Roz has received numerous awards and honours, including an MBE. She openly states that she wished to be of service to humankind, and this is her way.

The following story about Diana Nyad is another example of personal challenge and a history-making feat.[18]

More Risk Taking - Diana Nyad

The bigger the challenge, the greater the sense of achievement. This is true of Diana Nyad. At the tender age of 64, and in the dark of night, in pain from being stung by jellyfish, choking on salt water while singing to herself, Diana just kept on swimming. This was her fourth and final attempt to finally achieve her lifetime goal, which was to swim the 110 miles from Cuba to Florida.

Most opportunities in life, if they are to be fulfilled, require a willingness to take a risk. Indeed, a worthwhile achievement is worthy of taking a risk. But always use your intuition.

> There are two types of risk – the calculated risk
> and the uncalculated risk. Each has its place
> in decision-making.
>
> ~Vicky McGahey~

> **Attribute in Reflective Action**
> **RISK**
>
> *How can we build risk into our daily lives?*
> **Simply ...**
> Take a risk! Give a hand to those in need
> **Also**
> Risking everything in the hope you are
> doing what is right and just
> **And**
> Ensure that you do so to serve others
> **Then**
> Never say never – it is your chance to shine

When taking a risk you can leap in headfirst without much thought or you could stop and reflect to weigh up the risk, warts and all! The gift of time given to reflection could lessen the chance of failure. And yet, failure itself may be the first step forward to success – you can learn from your mistakes.

At times, suspending one's judgment would seem a wise thing to do. Hence the need for the fifth key Leadership Attribute of *Judgment*.

Chapter 8

JUDGMENT

with the satellite attribute of **Diversity**

Be curious, not judgmental.
Walt Whitman

Be not hasty in judging one another.
Mary MacKillop

Motto – suspend judgment; accept diversity and change

Symbol – scale

Suspending judgment requires detachment and reflection time. Dreher (1997) speaks of the Tao as defining detachment through this simple verse:

> The best leader does not use force ...
> The best managers seek to understand their people.
> This is the practice of detachment
> Which brings the power to lead others
> And is the highest lesson under heaven. (Tao, 68)
> **(Dreher, 1997)**[1]

Indeed, the art to judgment is being able to suspend it. Suspending judgment allows one to become aware of perceived notions of both the listener and the one seeking to be listened to.

Through detachment and the willingness to suspend judgment a leader can call upon their thoughts and feelings through reflective practice to recall the principles, values and other attributes that are needed to make a good decision.[2] John Dewey (1933) believed that we learn more from reflection upon a learning experience than the actual experience itself.[3]

The Leadership Attribute of *Diversity* is the satellite attribute of *Judgment*. It is discussed later within this chapter.

Daniel Goleman (1995) speaks of suspending judgment and empathy as key components of emotional intelligence.[4] Therefore, the leader should give themselves and others the 'gift of time', in order to reveal the wisdom of the experience. When detachment and suspension of judgment become custom and practice, a leader can listen to all points of view without the need to judge (at least straight away). This attribute allows for the redemptive side of community life to prevail (and team building to thrive). We are all in need of forgiveness from time to time.

In other words, the insight gained through reflection on our experiences from multiple perspectives can only occur through detachment and time. Taking time to listen to one's heart and soul (personal principles and values) for the answers to problems is a desirable attribute for a leader. Finding the gift of time to listen to the voices of others is another desirable leadership trait. Both of these traits require detachment, reflection and action.

More elaborately expressed by Killion and Todnem (1991), reflection is:

> A gift we give ourselves, not passive thought that lolls aimlessly in our minds, but an effort we must approach with rigour, with some purpose in mind, and in some formal way, so as to reveal the wisdom embedded in our experience. Through reflection, we develop context – specific theories that further our own understanding of our work and generate knowledge to inform future practice.[5]

As previously stated, one of Lincoln's most quotable quotes is 'judge not, that ye be not judged.' Lincoln had learnt through experience that harsh criticisms only lead to further rebuke and resentment.

As you reflect upon the attribute of judgment, review the following questions and jot down your thoughts. In doing so, you are engaging in a practice that will enrich your personal judgment.

1. Why is judgment an important attribute for one to develop within themself? As a leader?
2. Have you ever been asked to suspend your judgment?
3. How hard is it to do? To step back? To get a bigger snapshot of what is going on? To stop the chatter going on in your own head?
4. Why is the 'willingness' to suspend judgment an important attribute to practise? Give examples/stories.
5. Do we have the right to make judgments on others? Yes or no? Why? Give examples/stories.
6. Who are the best people to judge others? Why? Give examples/stories.
7. Where does empathy and compassion fit into judgment? Why? Give examples and stories.

There are times in life when we make judgments without checking all the facts because we react instead of being proactive. This can mean stopping and taking the time to consider. In time, through hindsight, we realise our mistake.

Have there been moments when, through stopping, reflecting and just letting things happen that what looks to be a tragedy, a travesty or a misfortune, now seems likely to be part of a bigger plan? Here is an example of just that – the story of the cuckoo. It is a modified version of a factual story written by Tali Landsman at her blog.[6]

Mutualism and Suspending Judgment – The Cuckoo

The cuckoo bird is not your average parent. In fact, they do their best to rid themselves of the responsibility of raising their young.

Cuckoo birds do not build a nest nor do they incubate their eggs. In the case of the great spotted cuckoo, they shrewdly place a single egg in the nests of other birds, particularly crows. The unsuspecting hosts sit on their own eggs and those of the cuckoo until the eggs hatch. Amazingly, they accept the fledgling that looks nothing like their own and become surrogate parents who raise the cuckoo as their own.

Why, may you ask? Recent studies on crows, including their nesting behaviours, found that those nests that had a cuckoo baby in them had a lower mortality rate. It seemed the crows' nests with a cuckoo in them were less susceptible to predators.

Scientists speculated with many different theories. One even suggested that the cuckoo parents had some psychic powers that allowed them to intuitively know which crows' nests were less susceptible to predators. With some perseverance, the truth was finally uncovered. The baby great spotted cuckoo secretes a repellent substance, with a vile smell that deters predators.

Scientists then decided to test this hypothesis. They fed fresh meat that was touched with this substance to hungry feral cats. They observed the feral cats turn away in disgust and refuse to come near it.

This species of so-called freeloading, sponging-off-others cuckoo turned out to be not just a trickster but also a saviour.

The willingness to suspend judgment is the essence of this attribute. It is the willingness that counts. One could say that the crows intuitively knew the presence of a cuckoo chick would increase the chances of survival for their own offspring. But they still had to be willing to wait and see – to suspend judgment. The same applies to we humans (sentient beings).

The Leadership Attributes Study supported the suspension of judgment through the time given to reflect upon principles, values and beliefs in relation to that judgment.[7]

The participants' responses encompassed two key concepts. These were:

- Suspend judgment.
- Reflection.

The Leadership Attributes Study revealed that the concept of judgment has its foundation within an individual at a personal level.

> It is a magnificent phrase (willingness to suspend judgment). I think that is sometimes where the truth often lies. It does not lie in my own perception of the truth – it lies somewhere in there (striking their chest thus indicating their own person). (Participant 8)

One participant felt that the willingness to suspend judgment was not enough. One needed to sit back and reflect.

> The willingness to suspend judgment – the explanation does not do justice to the concept I am trying to explain. This implies a huge amount of reflection. (Participant 2)

For some participants, it meant having the opportunity to first seek to understand. One participant spoke of the need to remain mindful: 'Mindfulness for me lets us be the fly on our roof all the time. In other words, watching yourself do things.' (Participant 2)

Another poignant point:

> Ideally, your attributes – in a position like I have – are all important. You should be suspending judgment until you have got the whole story. (Participant 1)

And, as also stated by the same participant:

You have got to allow time for yourself, for your head to get around it. And reflection is important in all we tend to do. We call it evaluation. We should really be calling it reflection. (Participant 1)

However, participants warned of the dangers of taking this attribute to its extreme:

I do not think you can suspend your own judgment in leadership. You might be unwilling to rush the judgment but you just cannot afford legally to step back from judgment. (Participant 4)

Your judgment must inform rather than be suspended. I would like to think of holding judgment off to the side rather then suspending it because sometimes in leadership you have got to deal with things which you personally would not in any place walk into but because you are dealing with other people you are – domestic violence, drugs, etc. (Participant 6)

Another potential problem is procrastination. Procrastination can be mistaken for detachment. It is important not to let procrastination set in and stifle any opportunity for creating shared meaning through open dialogue. Open and honest communication is essential.

There is another bird story to share from Tali Landsman.[8] It is a sad but inspiring story of the need to look below the surface at times … to step back and suspend our judgment. The following is an adapted version of Tali's story, which is further enhanced by research findings.[9]

Sacrifice and Suspending Judgment – The Snow Geese

Butte in Montana, USA, was once a mining boom-town, known as 'The Richest Hill in the World.' The legacy of those days has left its scars on the landscape and the environment – mining rigs dominate the scenery and the smell of sulphur permeates the air. In the hills surrounding the town there was an open-pit copper mine. Though the mine had been closed down for a number of years, over time, the pit had filled with water contaminated with toxic and corrosive run-off. The acid-filled 'lake' bubbled with its deadly toxins, getting worse each year, and it appeared that nothing was going to be done or even could be done.

A few years ago, 342 beautiful and graceful snow geese were tired from their long migration flight and needed to rest and seek food. They saw the lake and landed upon it. Their snow-white bodies were in sharp contrast to the red colour of the water. The geese drank the water and died. Their bodies floated for days, dead upon that water. A local vet carried out a post-mortem and discovered that the toxic water had virtually melted their throats, oesophagi and intestines.

Scientists were eventually employed to try to clean up the toxic mess. They were unsuccessful. However, one day, a scientist discovered a piece of debris floating in the lake. It was covered with slime, and this slime was alive! This was the first form of life to be found in this deadly water for years.

As the scientists continued their studies, they found that the organism thrived on the toxic water. But how? Further investigation revealed the truth. The slime was able to digest, remove and separate the toxins from the water. This was seen as a miracle. But it posed another question. How did the organism make it into the deadly lake? Through some serious investigative work, scientists discovered that the slimy organism can only be found in the intestine of snow geese.

Is it possible that the sacrifice of the geese had led to new life? That deadly pit now supports microorganisms, several of which have led to potential cures for ovarian cancer and tumours in the lungs.

Though nature may suffer at the hands of humankind, if given the gift of time, it may find a way to heal itself and restore that which was lost – and potentially create new life that can help existing life through new medicines and cures.

Therefore, be willing to suspend judgment so that the gift of time can weave its lessons into the fabric of our lives. And,

Comment often but judge little.

~Vicky McGahey~

> **Attribute in Reflective Action**
> **JUDGMENT**

How can we build judgment into our daily lives?

Simply ...

Stop! Suspend judgment

Also

Listen to understand and then
speak to be understood

And

Reflect! Honour the gift of reflection

Then

Make a decision

After significant analysis of the Leadership Attributes, the satellite attribute of *Diversity* was found to be directly related to the key Leadership Attribute of *Judgment*.

… Judgment

Diversity

> Diversity within unity; unity through diversity.
> **Vicky McGahey**

> Strength lies in differences, not in similarities.
> **Stephen Covey**

Motto – suspend judgment; accept diversity and change

Symbol – scale

Diversity is a strength! Diversity is what creates opportunity. Our diversity is our uniqueness. No two people, born of natural means, are exactly alike. It is our differences as individuals that create life-giving diversity that has an impact on survival and the continuance of life as we know it.

Suspending judgment while contemplating the diversity of a situation is essential. The long-term survival of any concept, organisation, community or family is its ability to embrace and harness diversity. Diversity can meet the challenges of constant change that has reached pandemic proportions in our world.

As the Leadership Attributes Study revealed: diversity within unity: unity through diversity.

The best team is always the most diverse team. It is the team with the most diverse talents and abilities. This can be largely due to the team's membership being made up of those who are thinkers and those who are doers, as well as those who are sequential in doing things and those who are quite random and unpredictable in their way of doing things. Diversity is a strength.

Research has shown that diversity is vital for cultural development. In the United States, over a ten-year period, the top 50 companies for diversity outperformed those not showing diversity by as much as 28%.[10]

A study of diversity in Fortune 1000 firms, found racial diversity among corporate leaders to be significantly related to revenues, net income, and to market equity. In Australia, the leadership ranks continue to lack gender and cultural diversity.[11] Employers are still failing to put adequate resources and strategies in place to drive change. Many companies have a policy about accepting diversity but the policy is not enough. Organisations need to properly resource and create a comprehensive strategy that includes clear objectives and real accountabilities. Organisations, whether business or community ignore the need for action in this area at their own peril.[12]

Therefore, a leader will seek out diversity and create the environment where diversity is accepted and encouraged as a means of signalling the possibility of change.

In the days of old, a shepherd (as a leader and protector of the flock) would not keep going back to regular feeding grounds as the flock grew – newer ground needed to be found. The wise shepherd also allowed the flock to interbreed. This ensured a healthy variety and diversity within the gene pool. There was less likelihood of genetic diseases and disorders. This is true of animal breeding in the world today.

As you reflect upon the attribute of diversity, consider the following questions and jot down your thoughts. In doing so, you are engaging in a practice that will enrich your personal judgment (diversity).

1. Why is diversity so important? Give examples/stories.
2. Why is diversity an important attribute for one to develop within themself? As a leader?
3. Diversity within unity; unity through diversity. What do you think about this statement? Give examples/stories.
4. In what ways is diversity good in team- and community-building practices? In what ways can diversity be bad in team- and community-building practices? Give examples/stories.
5. When interacting with a person from another culture, how do you ensure that communication is effective?
6. Have you ever had to work with someone who had a polar opposite personality to your own? How did you cope? Give examples/stories.
7. Give an example of how you walk in the shoes of people we serve and those with whom we work?

8. Give an example of a time when you could not be tolerant of another person's point of view. Why?
9. Have you ever been in a situation where your opinion was not recognised or just pushed aside? How did you feel?

There is a uniquely Australian story about an apple. This is a modified rendition of a story told by Bill Beatty in *A Treasury of Australian Folklore*.[13]

Granny Smith Apple – Maria Smith

The Granny Smith apple is no ordinary apple – its uniqueness was recognised by a woman named Maria Smith. It was different in colour, texture and taste and was a great cooking apple. Her ability to recognise the difference and her patience to test and develop the diverse characteristics of this apple is legendary.

Sadly, little has been done to honour the memory of a woman who developed and marketed an entirely new variety of apple. The Granny Smith apple has been described as the world's most valuable apple. It has exceptional taste, is an excellent cooking apple and stores extremely well. It is now universally acclaimed.

There are a number of stories associated with the original finding and cultivation of the first Granny Smith apple tree. The most acclaimed was published in a local paper, *Farmer and Settler*, on 25 June 1924. Nonetheless, the following is a brief and summarised version of those accounts.

Maria Smith came to Australia from England with her husband and five children in 1838. She had 16 children in her lifetime – most died in childbirth. Her only memorial is her tombstone at St Anne's Church in Ryde, which overlooks the Parramatta River.

It is reported that her husband was not a well man and most of the business and running of their farm rested with Maria. The farm was in Eastwood, near Ryde. When her fruiting trees were in season and with plenty of other farm produce, she would set up a stall in the city markets of Sydney.

It was during such a trip to the city markets that Maria bought a case of French crab apples from Tasmania. On finding the last of these in the case had gone bad, she tipped them out down by the creek course that ran through the family property.

From a seed that germinated, a new fruit tree grew up along the creek course. Maria knew that this was not a French crab-apple tree and was distinctly different to any other apple she had seen. She realised that she had something that was very different, very diverse and special.

In 1868, she called in Mr E. H. Small, a local orchardist and horticulturist, to give his opinion of her seeding apple tree. He passed his verdict and identified it as a new variety. Apples during this period were categorised either as being good for eating raw or as those to be used for cooking. He believed it to be quite a remarkable apple and the best cooking apple in Australia.

Maria seized the opportunity and began to market her new apple. She was then 69 years of age. She propagated the new variety, applying to it all her wisdom and a lifetime of growing apples. Soon, the fruit was taken down to the markets by Maria, or 'Granny' as she had become respectfully known. All her boxes and crates were marked with 'From Granny Smith's farm'. It is from these markings that the apple derived its name, and this new variety became an immediate favourite.

Maria was now known as Granny Smith. Soon she found fellow orchardists were keen to grow the new apple. She died 2 years later at 71 years of age.

Fortunately, her new, different, multi-use and diverse apple was so widely acclaimed in those first years it is now as close to a national treasure as it can be.

As a leader, you need to be able to accept that all differences are not bad – they are opportunities; to be able to see diversity as a strength and recognise difference and diversity within other people.

The study on Leadership Attributes supported this claim.[14] Leaders should encourage a community to suspend their judgment when faced with people or objects that are different or unfamiliar. Leaders need to help the community see that differences or diversity are a means for open dialogue towards finding shared values and purpose, for sometimes 'it is good to have a renegade in there who is going to question what I am doing, to challenge me' (Participant 10).

Diversity and differences are tools for creating unity and generating life within a community:

> A leader needs to take hold of issues and have a positive view. To sense where a community is in the scale of things and bring it back to life. Finding good in people to counteract the negativity and to see diversity as a strength, not a weakness. (Participant 4)

Several of the participants in the study indicated that diversity is an under-utilised strength.[15] Leaders are encouraged to build leadership teams that have people who display different talents, gifts, skills and knowledge. Indeed, it is through continuous dialogue that acknowledges and encourages diversity of opinion to be shared that new 'synergetic' realities are being born.

> Being able to suspend judgment: I put this one here because it is something I need to work on ... emotions. I am very quick to judge. I think a good leader needs to be able to see things from many different perspectives or points of views. A three-dimensional view of what life is all about. (Participant 3)

The following words of Marianne Williamson offer a profound wisdom.[16]

Words of Insight - Marianne Williamson

A woman of modern times is Marianne Williamson. She is known as a spiritualist and has become a well-known self-help guru. One of her most cited comments was incorrectly attributed to Nelson Mandela in his inaugural speech as President of South Africa.

> Our deepest fear is not that we are inadequate. Our deepest fear is that we are powerful beyond measure. It is our light, not our darkness that most frightens us. We ask ourselves, 'Who am I to be brilliant, gorgeous, talented, and fabulous'? Actually, who are you not to be? You are a child

of God. Your playing small does not serve the world. There is nothing enlightened about shrinking so that other people won't feel insecure around you. We are all meant to shine, as children do. We were born to make manifest the glory of God that is within us. It is not just in some of us; it is in everyone. And as we let our own light shine, we unconsciously give other people permission to do the same. As we are liberated from our own fear, our presence automatically liberates others.

Do not be afraid of your differences – instead, celebrate them. Seek differences in others and together celebrate the diversity of each other.

> Our differences are what make us unique.
> To be different, gifted with many talents,
> is a call to lead.
>
> ~Vicky McGahey~

And always remember:

> Diversity creates opportunity.
>
> ~Vicky McGahey~

> **Attribute in Reflective Action**
> **DIVERSITY**
>
> *How can we build diversity into our daily lives?*
> **Simply ...**
> Do not be afraid of your differences and the
> differences of others ... it is what
> makes us unique
> **Also**
> Seek diversity within unity; unity through diversity
> **And**
> Surround yourself with people who
> think differently to you
> **Then**
> Be the difference

There is a need for leaders to suspend judgment so that reflective practices that acknowledge change, difference and diversity can flourish. Once completed, a decision will have to be made. Then, once made, the decision will need to be communicated in a manner that ensures all concerned hear the same message. Hence the need for the sixth key Leadership Attribute of *Communication*.

Chapter 9

COMMUNICATION

with the satellite attribute of **Consistency**

COMMUNICATION

Consistency

Seek first to understand; then to be understood.
Stephen Covey

When people talk, listen completely.
Most people never listen.
Ernest Hemingway

Motto – be still and listen

Symbol – pen and voice

Communication

We should always be willing to develop and open lines of communication. This key attribute stresses the need to communicate openly with people through whatever medium is thought to be best (voice, written and action). In his book *Amplifiers*, Matt Church describes six modes of communication.[1] These are speaker, author, trainer, mentor, facilitator and coach. Each mode is important and we should seek to develop a skill set across these modes. Church suggests that we should deliver our messages across all these modes.

Essentially, we need to take the time to listen.[2] However, leaders often fail to communicate through lack of knowledge or skill, but if there is the will or intent to communicate, then one can assume that some action will be taken to rectify a problem.

This attribute is closely linked to another key attribute – empathy (the art of listening and feeling). The Leadership Attribute of *Consistency* is the satellite attribute of *Communication*. It is discussed within this chapter.

The art and profession of herding animals dates back to early humankind and the formation of community. The tradition and many practices have not changed in thousands of years. The shepherd would develop and train the flock by the use of signals and sounds. These sounds would warn the flock of danger, and the need to regroup or split up. In the morning, each shepherd would gather his flock through a distinctive guttural sound and lead them to their own feeding grounds. The shepherd would become familiar with the sights and sounds of the flock as they communicated with each other. The shepherd would take the time to listen.[3]

As you reflect upon the attribute of communication, review the following questions and jot down your thoughts. In doing so, you are engaging in a practice that will enrich your personal communication.

1. Why is communication an important attribute for one to develop within themself? As a leader?
2. In times of struggle, how willing are you to communicate with someone you have an issue with? Do you just avoid any

communication or do you actively seek engagement to resolve the issue? Be honest here. Give examples/stories.
3. Do I hear and understand the other person? Do I respect the other person's opinions? What are some ways to stop the chatter in your head, to really seek to hear, to hear what is being said to you?
4. Do I take responsibility for what is being understood by the listener? Am I being understood correctly? Why is this important? Give examples/stories.
5. How do I add value to the conversation I am having with those I agree with? Disagree with?

Have you ever tried to stop the chatter in your head when someone else is talking to you? To really shut up and shut out that noise that blocks you from really listening to the other person. It seems most people ask a question, wait a microsecond for a person to answer and then straight away start to think of what to say next. Therefore, not really listening to the response being given by another.

To really listen requires the ability to shut off the chatter in one's head as you listen to another speak. This ability takes time to master and is an essential leadership skill. The following story from Rachel Naomi Remen will reveal this.[4]

Just Listen

Rachel Naomi Remen speaks of listening as the most basic and powerful way to connect to another person, especially if it's done from the heart. As a doctor, she treats many people with cancer. She no longer hands out tissues to crying patients for she found it was just another way to shut them down, to take them out of their experience of sadness and grief, which they need to experience so that they can move on. So now she just listens. When they have cried all they need to cry, they find her there with them.

The Leadership Attributes Study revealed a person who had overcome this inability to really listen.[5]

Communication

Listen! Really Listen – 'Marian'

Marian (not her real name), was one of the people interviewed in the Leadership Attributes Study. She was the director of a large educational office with numerous schools – both primary and secondary – under her leadership.

People really cared about her because she really cared about them. As one participant said:

> You know when she talks to you – you feel you are the most important person in the room. Marian gives you her full attention. She really makes an effort to see things from your perspective. Marian really listens and sincerely tries to empathise with you.

Remember, the most powerful way to connect with another person is to listen – to just listen. Often we interrupt so as to let the person know we understand. But all we do is focus attention on ourselves. The next time someone is talking to you, just stop the chatter in your head. Reaffirm them by just listening and make sure you are still there when they have finished. See the difference that your listening can make to a person's reality. You too become known for your ability to make people feel they are the most important person in the room.

The gift of silence can create an atmosphere that allows healing and connection – 'silence speaks for itself.' As Rachel Naomi Remen stated: 'A loving silence often has far more power to heal and connect than the most well-intentioned words.'[6]

The Leadership Attributes Study revealed that communication is an essential leadership skill.[7] As an attribute, it is the 'willingness to communicate' – to be prepared to listen to the voice of others through open and honest dialogue.

The participants' responses surrounded several key concepts. These were:

- listen (willingness to listen)
- wisdom (shared)
- stories.

As the participants stated: 'True communication is listening to others.' (Participant 7)

Communication between a leader or leaders and a community is essential for the genesis, which in this instance implies re-birthing, and the growth of a community. It is the continuous sharing of principles, values and beliefs that is the essence of establishing community. Effective communication is dependent upon the degree of willingness to communicate. If there is not an honest desire to communicate, then effective communication will not eventuate and community-building practices cannot evolve.

Communication is seen as more than just speaking and getting the message across. It is the seeking and sharing of knowledge from each other (wisdom sharing). As the participants expressed:

> Articulate a vision which several other people can walk along with – this is very important. Going along with this is a very strong need to have an extraordinary sense of communication – of being able to share that with other people and invite other people to share with you. (Participant 6)

> When we do find that there is a willingness to communicate then the truth that we did not know what existed becomes more transparent and, in that way, I feel more comfortable and then the other person feels more comfortable. We are all working towards the same thing anyway ... the willingness to communicate. (Participant 3)

> It is a great affirmation of the other person to mutually seek or to explain something that is puzzling you. I think that is a lovely mind. (Participant 8)

Therefore, leaders should employ strategies that ensure all voices are heard:

> Everyone has got something special to bring. I make sure everyone gets their chance to talk and that we acknowledge the contribution of everyone and all that builds up a sense of community. (Participant 10)

Communication

> A leader should be willing to speak out for those who do not have a voice. I am often asked to speak for those that don't have a voice in circles of policy and so on. That is seen as very important in my job – I see it as important in my job. That no matter what is being discussed that you come to that forum from the perspective of those that are not being represented in that particular forum – so that notion of compassion is important. (Participant 3)

Participants spoke of communities and teams as having ritual, celebration and shared stories that embody what community is. It is up to the leader to create and foster many of these stories and rituals so as to communicate the true purpose of the community.

> The symbol, myth and ritual place that the sharing of this togetherness and being a part of ordinary spoken word and the ordinary things that are done … the *stories* – that is part of the community and therefore that sense of how we celebrate one another. (Participant 6)

> His speech captured the essence of what we had just done – it was brilliant. He used a huge amount of symbolism that developed into ritual. (Participant 10)

Several participants spoke of the need for a leader to communicate in order to build community. However, communication is more than just the willingness to communicate, for 'leaders have to be able to communicate, otherwise they cannot do the essential things of being community … if you cannot communicate you cannot build the levels of understanding – to have people share common values.' (Participant 4)

This view was shared by many participants, who spoke of a leader's ability to articulate their values and beliefs. Much of this articulation is achieved through example, or modelling – an essential activity for every leader to exercise regularly.

Here is a fabled example of a leader not taking modelling seriously.[8]

Modelling – Military Section Leader

A man in civilian clothes rode past a small group of exhausted, battle-weary soldiers digging an obviously important defensive position. The section leader, making no effort to help, was shouting orders and threatening punishment if the work was not completed within the hour.

'Why are you are not helping?' asked the stranger on horseback.

'I am in charge. The men do as I tell them,' said the section leader, adding, 'Help them yourself if you feel strongly about it.'

To the section leader's surprise, the stranger dismounted and helped the men until the job was finished. Before leaving, the stranger congratulated the men for their work, and approached the puzzled section leader.

'You should notify top command next time your rank prevents you from supporting your men – and I will provide a more permanent solution,' said the stranger.

Up close, the section leader now recognised the helpful stranger. It was the king.

The wise use of analogies and examples is vital when communicating. This was an approach used extensively by Rear Admiral Grace Hopper of the US Navy Reserve.[9]

Wise Use of Analogies – Rear Admiral Grace Hopper

Grace Hopper is an example of a great leader and communicator. She led a distinguished career as an academic, in industry and in the military. Rear Admiral Hopper displayed numerous talents, had outstanding technical skills and repeatedly demonstrated her business and political acumen. She never gave up on her good ideas and she was prepared to talk to people.

Her use of analogies and examples was legendary. Once, she presented a piece of wire about a foot long, and explained that it represented a nanosecond, since it was the maximum distance electricity could travel along wire in one-billionth of a second.

Communication

Admiral Hopper believed her greatest contribution had been the knowledge she shared with the young people she had trained. As an inspirational professor and a much sought-after speaker in the latter years of her life, she addressed more than 200 audiences.

Her work spanned programming languages, software development concepts, compiler verification and data processing. Her early recognition of the potential for commercial applications of computers, and her leadership and perseverance in making this vision a reality, paved the way for modern data processing.

What a team Grace Hopper and Ada Lovelace (see Chapter 7) would have made! Both computer pioneers – Ada, the founding mother of data processing, and Grace, the loyal advocate and master of modern data processing.

> Be still!
> Listen to the silent voices.
> Silence speaks for itself.
> ~Vicky McGahey~

> **Attribute in Reflective Action**
> **COMMUNICATION**

How can we build better communication into our daily lives?

Simply ...

Listen! Then talk

Also

Stop the chatter in your own head

while listening intently

And

Listen to the silent voice, your own and others,

for silence speaks for itself

Then

Be silent

After significant analysis of the Leadership Attributes, the satellite attribute of *Consistency* was found to be directly related to the key Leadership Attribute of *Communication*.

Effective communication is delivered in a manner that ensures consistency of message to all concerned and across all platforms.

Consistency

> Consistency is the foundation of virtue.
> **Francis Bacon**

> The secret of success is constancy of purpose.
> **Benjamin Disraeli**

Motto – be still and listen

Symbol – pen and voice

As individuals, we often feel the need to be consistent in our principles, values and beliefs. Some view consistency as making things easy.[10] Once faced with something you have had to deal with, you never have to think of it again. In every new situation, just apply the old consistent thinking or rule of thumb. But consistency means so much more. This is particularly true of consistency when in a leadership role.

Consistency is a sense that someone is 'always there'. The person who is always there to offer support and guidance to all in need, including those who have done us wrong. Forgiveness and the opportunity for redemption are a necessary action for all leaders to display. Indeed, forgiveness and redemption can be considered a hallmark for leadership that is moral.

Consistency within this context does not mean doing everything the same every time. It means being consistent in your treatment of people. This is particularly significant when dealing with people's needs or perceived needs.

A leader will always attend to the needs of the community. They will know each member by name and tend to their individual needs. They will listen and, in this way, endeavour to treat them as equals.

As you reflect upon the attribute of consistency, consider the following questions and jot down your thoughts. In doing so, you are engaging in a practice that will enrich your personal communication (consistency).

1. Why is being consistent important? Give examples/stories.
2. Why is consistency an important attribute for one to develop within themselves? As a leader?
3. How often do you notice the inconsistencies of others? Why? Give examples/stories. (Remember – it is sometimes easier to see the splinter in the eyes of others than it is to see the log in your own eyes [the splinter and the log are faults]).
4. What has consistency got to do with commitments? Making commitments? Why? Give examples/stories.
5. Why are consistent actions more important then consistent words? Or are they?
6. How do you ensure consistent communication with all people? Why is this important?

The following story, told in many forms, is one of those stories whose message can be of many things.[11] This version has an Australian twist.

The Kangaroo and the Echidna

One day, a kangaroo and echidna were walking and talking along a bush track. The kangaroo began making fun of the echidna for his slowness.

The echidna was annoyed, but said with a smile, 'I may be slow, but I can beat you in a race.'

The kangaroo was astonished to hear this. He thought the echidna was utterly foolish to suggest that he could beat the kangaroo.

'Are you kidding?' said the kangaroo trying to contain his laughter, for he did not wish to offend. 'I hope you are not serious.'

'I am very serious. I am sure I can beat you in a race,' said the echidna.

Seeing the echidna so serious, the kangaroo said, 'All right, let's have a race!'

They agreed to visit their friend the emu and ask him to referee, which he obligingly agreed to do. A large field had just been cleared of its crop. The field ran beside a river and at the end was a giant gum tree. The emu guessed the tree was more than a kilometre away, so it became the winning post.

Communication

'On your mark, get set, go,' called the emu, and the race began.

The kangaroo took off at lightning speed, and soon hopped out of sight towards the finish line. Meanwhile, the echidna began the race at a very slow pace.

'Poor echidna,' thought the emu, 'the kangaroo will win the race hands down. No match at all!'

When the kangaroo reached the halfway point, he stopped to see where the echidna was. When he looked back, the echidna was nowhere to be seen.

'Oh! He is far behind, I can't even see him yet. I think I will wait here until I can see him and then I'll hop the remaining distance. Hey, why don't I eat some of the hay and grass. I can rest for a while,' said the kangaroo to himself.

The kangaroo ate and drank from the river. He lay down in the shade of a bottlebrush tree to wait and watch. Soon, the cool air from the riverside lulled him into a deep sleep. The echidna on the other hand, kept moving slowly but steadily.

The kangaroo slept for a long time. When he woke up, he looked around ... and the echidna was still nowhere to be seen. The kangaroo felt rested and so decided to complete the race. As he approached the finish line, he could see the echidna. The echidna had already crossed the finish line.

The kangaroo had lost the race. He accepted the defeat graciously. After that he never poked fun at the echidna or his slowness.

The moral of the story is simple. Consistency, persistence, determination and a belief in oneself will always win the day. The echidna showed that if you have all that you need to win the race, the only thing that could stop you from winning the race is lack of persistence and consistency in effort. Meanwhile, the kangaroo learnt that ability is one thing, but it is useless if not applied consistently.

So what is consistency?

The Leadership Attributes Study revealed several ideas on just what consistency means.[12]

> Consistency means knowing were the end is. Then doing a little bit every moment no matter how slow till you reach your goal. A steady pace will ensure you reach the end even if it is slow. It did not matter what others are able to do or not able to do, goal achievement means that you should be consistent in your efforts to achieve your goal. In reality, what you do slowly, steadily, day in and day out will make achieving your goals effortless. (Participant 6)

The Leadership Attributes Study revealed consistency is an important attribute to foster in one's actions. Consistency in effort can achieve remarkable things. One significant response from a participant in the study really hit home:

> It is not that hard to come up with moral values, it is consistency in living them. That is what is difficult. It is hard for yourself to apply moral rules. We are very bad at living up to them (values). People rationalise and make excuses for themselves and their community and we are actually very bad when it comes to being critical or moral in our own case. (Participant 7)

Here is another story (with yet another Australian twist) about being consistent.[13] However, it has a negative connotation. Do not expect change in those who, by their very nature, will not change. Watch for those who have predictable and consistent behavioural patterns.

The Scorpion and the Platypus

One day, a scorpion looked around his desert home and decided that he wanted a change. So he set out on a journey to find a billabong or a waterhole he could live by. But it was the rainy season, and much of the flat lands, roads and byways were filled with water.

As he came to a wide and swift-running waterway, the scorpion stopped on dry land to reconsider the situation. He couldn't see any way across. So he ran up and down, all the while thinking that he might have to turn back.

Communication

Suddenly, he saw a platypus sitting in the rushes by the bank of the ever-widening stream. He decided to ask the platypus for help in getting across the stream.

'Hello, Mr Platypus!' called the scorpion, 'Would you be so kind as to give me a ride on your back across these waters?'

'Well now, Mr Scorpion! How do I know that if I try to help you, you won't sting me and kill me?' asked the platypus.

'Because,' the scorpion replied, 'if I try to kill you, then I would die too, for, you see, I cannot swim!'

The platypus took pity on the scorpion and his plight, for the waters were beginning to rise around the ever-decreasing bank of land where the scorpion was taking refuge.

'Come on then,' cried the platypus.

The scorpion crawled onto the platypus's back, his sharp claws pricking in the platypus's fur, and the platypus slid into the rising waters. The muddy water swirled around them, but the platypus stayed near the surface so that the scorpion would not drown. He moved strongly through the waters, against the current, heading towards higher ground.

When nearly at their destination, the platypus suddenly felt a sharp sting in his back and, out of the corner of his eye, saw the scorpion remove his stinger. A deadening numbness began to creep into his limbs.

'You fool!' cried the platypus, 'Now we shall both die! Why on earth did you do that?'

The scorpion shrugged, and smiled back. 'I could not help myself. It is my nature.'

Then, they both sank into the muddy waters of the swiftly flowing waters, never to be seen again.

Upon quiet reflection, one can see that the platypus displayed many of the attributes we aspire to develop within ourselves, such as the willingness to suspend judgment and take a risk. The platypus also showed trust and was empathetically compassionate to the scorpion's plight. However, he forgot to take into account the true nature of the scorpion (the beast before him). This led the platypus on a path towards self-destruction – a very real threat that can cheat us out of what we seek and are trying to achieve for ourselves and for others. The secret is to watch out for the predictable behaviours of others and act accordingly.

'It's my nature,' said the scorpion. How pathetic! Of course it was! Frankly, make sure you are not a scorpion or the unprepared platypus ... if you are the scorpion, seek ways to diminish your sting; if you are the platypus, carry a life jacket and be prepared. 'Practice makes perfect' is a popular and widely used saying. It is definitely true for the development of consistency within oneself. Therefore,

> **Be consistent in all things. Treat others equitably, including oneself.**
>
> ~Vicky McGahey~

Communication

> **Attribute in Reflective Action**
> **CONSISTENCY**

How can we build consistency into our daily lives?

Simply ...
Be you

Also
Become yourself through consistent
growth and change

And
Be the best you can be for yourself and others

Then
Become yourself and grow in wisdom
founded in courage and conviction
for what is right

Moving on ...

The following chapter will present the leadership attributes in action, as given in the published paper on The Shepherd Metaphor for leadership (see Appendix C). These are the action steps in which the attributes can be given life. They have been revised and modified to suit the nature and intent of this book. The Shepherd Metaphor does have a distinct religious connotation about it. Indeed, that was my intent. However, this book is not intended only for those who have a religious leaning, but is also inclusive of those who seek to learn, lead, and build communities that are good.

For:

> Goodness is a natural calling – it is in our DNA.
> ~Vicky McGahey~

We are all born good within our soul, but to be a good person is only a desire of the heart unless we choose to be good.

~Vicky McGahey~

Chapter 10

The Leadership Attributes in Action

The Leadership Attributes, as described in the previous chapters, are essential ingredients for becoming a leader.

- A leader will have followers and be a follower themselves.
- A leader will build a team of leaders and therefore establish community.
- A leader will make a difference.
- A leader will care enough to stop and listen to the voice within and the voices surrounding them.
- A leader will be willing to accept change through consistent effort to continually improve and grow their community – be that an organisation, local group or family.

But, there needs to be a strategy so that this good community building and moral leadership can be put into action. I believe such a strategy can be found in the following words:

A graceful vision of a grace-filled mission is a call to action.

A vision and a mission are worthless without some actioning taking place. Sadly, many vision and mission statements end up as a plaque or a picture on a wall … and that is where it begins and ends. The Leadership Attributes are a call to action or, at the very least, can be a tool to help facilitate that action.

The Leadership Attributes Study, as described throughout the leadership attributes in the previous chapters, was born from a simple metaphor for leadership. The metaphor describes a leader in action as being a shepherd. A shepherd will lead from the front, occasionally pushing from behind, but mainly walks within and, therefore, with their community. This metaphor is called The Shepherd Metaphor (Appendix C).

There are three strategic action components to The Shepherd Metaphor of leadership. These are:

- gathering
- pathfinding
- presence.

Gathering is essential to secure followership. You're not a leader without followers. Therefore, gathering relies on the leader's vision and mission to draw followers: leadership within followership; followership through leadership.

Once gathered, it is essential that the leader's vision and mission point towards an achievable path and become a shared vision and mission.

Finally, the team and community need to always feel the leader's presence ... that he or she will always be there.

The following sections will briefly describe the three strategic action components.

1. GATHERING – VISION AND MISSION

> The Tao leader creates harmony
> Reaching
> From the heart
> To build community. (Tao, 49)
>
> **(Dreher, 1997)**[1]

The gathering action is what leads to the formation of a community. The attribute of integrity features strongly here – the integrity of the leader and the integrity of those following. A leader's vision, mission and plan are tools that can be used to gather people and gain the support needed for the establishment of a community. A leader would use their vision and mission to inspire others to gather and to create a sense of belonging and unity – they are the prophets of hope. This gathering will grow into a community of collective minds – very diverse, all different and unique.

Leadership need not be the role of one person within a community or organisation. Different members of a community can assume the role of being a leader at different times. Different circumstances can often require a different mindset and skills. Indeed, all members of the community should aspire to be leaders. In this way, the single vision and mission can become a shared vision and mission for the community. This is achieved through open dialogue surrounding the vision and mission of the community or organisation. In this way the gathering community creates a shared graceful vision of a grace-filled mission, which is a call to action.

Once gathered, the flock needs to be directed and guided towards green pastures and a safe resting place. Leaders will become the pathfinders.

2. PATHFINDING – GUIDE FOR THE JOURNEY

> Leaders must have the courage to follow their vision (shared), to believe in the invisible, to work for something that is still only a possibility, while others often wring their hands in despair.
>
> (Dreher, 1997)[2]

Leaders should seek new paths and new directions in which the vision and mission can flourish and be transformed into action. They need to become pathfinders.[3]

As stated several times, a graceful vision of a grace-filled mission is a call to action. To act upon a shared vision and mission requires the use of emotional intelligence and development of intrapersonal and interpersonal skills.[4] Such action can create a steep learning curve in people, which will involve the use of inner energy, spirit and emotion.[5] This emotion can be harvested and used wisely. For, as Goleman (1996) states:

> Being able to motivate oneself and persist in the face of frustrations; to control impulse and delay gratification; to regulate one's moods and keep distress from swamping the ability to think; to empathise and to hope.[6]

These abilities take time to develop within a person. They require a degree of self-awareness, authenticity, transparency, resilience, empathy with other's perspectives, tolerance, acceptance of differences and the will to seek to build authentic grace-filled and trusting relationships. To be a pathfinder, a person needs to be willing to adopt actions that display flexibility, adaptability, openness to new ideas and practices, accountability, ingenuity and innovativeness.[7]

As a pathfinder, the leader will need to find within themselves the attributes of passion, faith as a belief in a bright value-led future and transcendence.[8] This will need to be a cornerstone and the foundation upon which a moral community is built. The pathfinders will also need to be willing to trust the community in shared decision-making.

Leadership, as defined in this book, comes from within – it is a knowing, a calling that speaks of goodwill, authenticity and presence through the sharing of insight and truth. It can be found in one's own intuition. It is leadership that views people as the most valuable resource and source of happiness. Therefore, leadership can be a shared reality.[9]

Different members of a community may step forward to be the leader depending on the terrain ahead. Leadership needs to be dynamic, as the context and task needs to change from event to event and situation to situation. This is why succession planning is so important. Succession needs to be planned, managed and people need to be taught and nurtured to take on leadership responsibilities, depending on the attributes and skills they bring to the community. It needs to be ongoing, with the net being cast out many times. Succession should never be narrowed down or limited to 'the one' in the community. Succession planning should begin on day one of any new leadership role or job. Likely candidates can be mentored, coached and nurtured for future leadership possibilities.

The leader is spiritual, a wanderer of open spaces, freedom and green pastures. The leader will mingle with the community – sometimes walking behind, sometimes at the front, but usually within the community. And as Lao Tzu taught, leaders are able to:

> Live with humility
> Remaining ahead of their people
> By walking behind. (Tao, 66)
>
> (Dreher, 1997)[10]

Therefore, leaders need to be always searching with passion, always seeing ahead and being guided by their intuitive heart and soul, and always believing in a bright future. Pathfinding will require some risk taking and leaders will need to become trailblazers that are living examples of the competencies and skills to be lived and taught.

A leader needs to evoke a vision that will guide a community to the greener pastures of tranquillity, satisfaction, protection and rest.[11]

3. PRESENCE – ALWAYS THERE

> A good shepherd never left his sheep alone.
> They would have been lost without him.
> His presence was their assurance.
>
> (Roper, 1997)[12]

The *Tao Te Ching* discloses:

> Without the One, the heavens would fall,
> The earth would die,
> The spirits would mourn,
> The valleys dry up. (Tao, 39)
>
> (Dreher, 1997)[13]

This action of presence – 'always being there' – is vital for developing endurance and perseverance within a community. A leader's presence should always be felt through their actions.

Leaders must be seen as trustworthy, fair and consistent. There is also a need for leaders to be willing to communicate openly and become:

The constant voice that calls for ethical commitment, vision, behaviour, achievement and courage ... someone must be the keeper of the corporate conscience. Someone must remind the organisation of the need to err on the side of goodness.[14]

Leaders will 'coach rather than control, mentor as well as manage, strengthen others, not just supervise their work, empower, not just employ.'[15] It is leadership that focuses on spirit rather than style or means. However, as previously stated, to define and measure spiritual growth remains a difficult and relatively little-researched paradigm.[16]

A leader knows their people by name and knows all the cuts and bruises they carry (empathy). Leaders should display compassion and caring that is open to all in need. Through a leader's actions, a leader's integrity shines forth.

Chapter 11

Summary and Conclusion

The end is in sight! It has come! Well at least for this book! In my introduction, I spoke of the quest and desire to find Camelot or at the very least find a way to create it. Without too much reflection, I realised the foundation stones could be the qualities or attributes that lie naturally within humans.

To reveal these attributes, we need to begin an introspective and retrospective journey of the heart, mind and soul. During this reflection and journey we will 'become' or at the very least be open to 'becoming' – to grow beyond that which we can imagine ourselves to be. In other words, to be a better person for oneself, others and the universe.

Chapter 1 discussed the old saying: leaders are born or leaders are made. An argument was given that hopefully convinced you that, indeed, leaders are born *and* leaders are made, regardless of gender. Sadly, the lack of women in leadership roles is still a tragedy and a shameful example of inaction by humankind. It is all the more tragic because the naturally soft nature of women blends so beautifully with the strong, supportive strength of men. We need the balance of gender in leadership, and it is not there yet.

The chapter also discussed the concept of leadership and what was wrong with leadership – the abuse of power.

To review: I proposed that there are four reasons why one becomes a leader:

- higher ideal
- domination
- chosen
- born.

Any one of these can be a reason for becoming a leader and, equally, all four may be inclusive in the actions of an individual or group at any given time. More importantly, I spoke of the reasons 'why' this book and its focus on leadership attributes is significant at this point in time. These included, but are not exclusive of:

1. Sensing the urgent need for good leadership in a troubled world and at every level of human existence. We live in disruptive times. World leaders struggle to cope with housing, finance, terrorism, nations at war, refugees and immigrants.
2. The need to establish communities that are essentially good and moral, where the foundation stones are tolerance and seeing diversity as a strength. Communities displaying these attributes need to exist in organisations, local groups and families.
3. The need for each of us to rise to the occasion and be the role models and, therefore, leaders within the family and the wider community – not just leaving it up to a few.
4. The need for women in leadership. The lack of a gender balance inhibits the growth and development of organisations, local groups and family life.
5. The need for leaders to develop the leadership attributes within themselves. They are a game-changer and can be a disruptive, provocative and challenging voice within that causes a shift in the sensing of oneself and purpose.

The reasons 'why' people follow are important points to consider in leadership – for you are not a leader without followers. As previously stated: leadership within followership; followership through leadership. There are three simple reasons 'why' we follow. These are:

- The person themself (attributes).
- The message they are telling (selling).
- The 'buy into' – what's in it for me/us (support).

Through research, it was revealed that the person themself and their personal attributes are the most significant reason/s to follow another person. Unfortunately, the issue of power and the need for individuals and groups to have control over others has been a plague upon humanity. However, as history has proven, dictatorship – whether by an individual or individuals – will come to an end. Sadly, more often than not, the end is a disaster not only for themself/themselves, but also for those they led. However, the need for ultimate power over another now presents a real threat to humankind. At no other time in world history have we been at a point when we could totally annihilate life as we know it.

To conclude Chapter 1, a number of general statements about leadership were made:

1. Leaders are born and leaders are made, regardless of gender.
2. Leadership is a call to service.
3. Leadership is first and foremost a personal journey. To be a good and wise leader begins and ends within.
4. Leadership is making use of the innate human attributes (leadership attributes) within us. These can be used to influence others to listen and follow. Each and every one of us has these leadership attributes.
5. Leadership is not a solo sport.
6. Leadership within followership; followership through leadership.
7. Leadership involves establishing relationships, which, in turn, establish community.
8. Leadership is persuasion.
9. Leadership is the transparent and authentic use of power.
10. Never allow the destination to become more important than the journey. The journey is where the lessons of life are learnt and those lessons are what make life unique, precious and good. So, be thankful and gracious in accepting the experiences and lessons of life.

Leadership viewed in this way will build a community that is essentially moral (good) and based upon principles, values and beliefs where life is cherished as the precious gift.

Summary and Conclusion

Chapter 2 expanded on the theme of 'becoming' through the telling of stories. Some stories were true, some were abstract, and there were at least one or two fables and a parable. The chapter ended with a list of key features to work on as one journeys on the road to 'becoming'. These include, but are not exclusive of:

1. What lies within us is most important.
2. Seek the answer to life's questions from within – what is felt is more important than what is thought.
3. Venture into your soul. Become aware of your attributes and gifts. Reflect upon these daily as Benjamin Franklin did.
4. Lead with grace – be generous, respectful, redemptive and make sacrifices.
5. Become a courageous model of transparency and authenticity. Be accountable.
6. Help others to find themselves and 'become'.
7. Never allow the destination to become more important than the journey. The journey is where the lessons of life are learnt and those lessons are what make life unique, precious and good. So, be thankful and gracious in accepting the experiences and lessons of life.

The main focus of this book is on leadership attributes, which are introduced in Chapter 3 and then featured in more detail in Chapters 4 to 9. Leadership attributes were born through research study on leadership, learning and building community. The presentation of the leadership attributes in each chapter hopefully met your needs through story, research findings and reflective questions.

The appendices, listed below, provide a more in-depth coverage of the concepts presented in the book:

- Appendix A   The Leadership Attributes
- Appendix B   The Conceptual Theories of the Leadership Attributes Study
- Appendix C   The Shepherd Metaphor
- Appendix D   *The Invitation* by Oriah Mountain Dreamer
- Appendix E   Benjamin Franklin's 13 Virtues

Conclusion

Thank you for the gift of your time in reading this book. I hope it will prove to be a valuable book that you come back to as you journey on the road to 'becoming' ... whatever that may be for you, your family, and your community.

Leaders are born and leaders are made. At some point in time, all of us will be called to lead. This can be in the smallest of situations or events of life. It is as simple as when someone asks us for advice or when we see a need that requires action. Leadership is service.

Hopefully, you find the time to reflect and will continue to do so. Indeed, taking each attribute one week at a time and reflecting upon it – in the manner of Benjamin Franklin and his 13 virtues – may be a good trait to develop. This can be achieved through a journal. A free journal is available as a companion to this book (available through my website: www.vickymcgahey.com).

Finally ... be ready! Have the leadership attributes well in place.

Summary and Conclusion

Leadership Attributes in Reflective Action
THE FIFTEEN LEADERSHIP ATTRIBUTES

How can we build the leadership attributes into our daily lives?

Simply ...

Be present through service

Also

Forgive and seek forgiveness. Practise redemption

often. It's all about relationships.

And

Always remember –

leadership within followership;

followership through leadership

Then

Be still, silent and listen

Appendix A

The Leadership Attributes

The following attributes have evolved from literature research and subsequent literature reviews in a Masters dissertation (1993) and a Doctorate thesis (2001) by this author. The areas of study included human resources management, leadership, moral community, teaching and learning. A reference list is given at the end of this appendix.

Since that time, the leadership attributes have been further developed and used in several models to describe the attributes required of a person, whether as a leader and/or as a follower. These attributes are what all people should aspire to develop within themselves and bring to life through their action(s).

The 15 attributes are given below. The six key attributes, and their associated satellite attributes are organised as they appear in this book.

1. Integrity

Integrity is being whole as the person you are; honest with yourself. Integrity is found in the quiet recesses of the heart and soul. It is nurtured by the time one spends reflecting upon personal principles and values and how these are best expressed in the living of life.

TRUST

To trust is to take a leap of faith. It is the willingness to trust that is essential. If you do not show a willingness to trust, how can you expect to be trusted?

TRUSTWORTHY

To be worthy of another's trust you must first show that you trust them. Those who do not show a willingness to trust others cannot expect to be trusted. It is a double-edged sword and trust is a two-way street.

2. Prophecy

There is a need for each of us, as individuals, to become prophets of our own future. This will take courage and the willingness to take a stand and to accept the challenge. In a world that experiences suffering and sorrow on a grand scale, now, more than ever, we need to be prophets of hope.

TRANSCENDENCE

Transcendence is our inherent awareness of our place in the world. It is purity and perfection, eminence and excellence, goodness and grace. It is a moment in time when one has a clear vision of the future that is energising and desired.

FAITH

Faith is the belief in oneself and the principles, values and beliefs one holds dear. Faith is also a belief in a future. Sometimes that future is not of our own making.

3. Empathy

We need to increase our empathy by taking the time to listen and immerse ourselves in the problems and issues of others. To endeavour to stop, cut off the chatter in our heads, and really feel for others.

COMPASSION

Compassion and courage go hand in hand. Compassion is often regarded as a sign of weakness, but, in fact, it takes great courage to be compassionate – to care and be patient. Compassion requires trust in oneself – in one's own intuitive judgment and wisdom. The act of compassion requires one to give of themselves and to shut out the endless chatter in their head!

PASSION

Passion is enthusiasm and persistence that flows from the heart. We can use this attribute to motivate people towards actions that will create and sustain a sense of community – a sense of belonging.

4. Intuition

Intuition is said to be an unconscious form of knowledge that rests just below the conscious level of thought. It is an inner voice – the direct perception of truth. The inner voice has long been regarded as one of the best tools for finding solutions to questions of purpose (life, personal and community direction).

RISK

Fear of the outcome of an action is the reason people are afraid to take risks. We should not worry about the outcome of our actions when the action is in line with our principles and values. It was Gandhi who believed that we are not responsible for the outcome. Our duty is to make sure that our motives are pure and our means are consistent with our beliefs. If we take care of our motives and means, the rest will follow naturally.

5. Judgment

The willingness to suspend judgment and to practise reflection while considering from different points of view is essential (multiple perspectives). Being able to suspend judgment requires detachment and reflection time. We do not actually learn from experience as much as we learn from reflecting on that experience.

DIVERSITY

Diversity is a strength! Our different traits and personalities can be used as strengths to build community. Our diversity is our uniqueness. Diversity is what creates opportunity. Diversity within unity: unity through diversity.

6. Communication

We need to communicate openly with people through whatever medium is thought to be best (voice, written, action). Take the time to listen. We often fail to communicate through a lack of knowledge or skill, but if there is the will or intent to communicate, then one can assume that some action will be taken.

CONSISTENCY

Within this context, consistency does not mean doing everything the same way every time. It means being consistent in one's treatment of people. Consistency is a sense that someone is 'always there'. People are quick to ascertain if a person is someone who is always there to offer support and guidance to all.

Bibliography

Bennis, W. & Nanus, B., *Leaders: The Strategies for Taking Charge*, Harper & Row, New York, 1985, p. 101.

Bezzina, M., 'Paying Attention to Moral Purpose in Leading Learning: Lessons from the Leaders Transforming Learning and Learners Project,' *Educational Management Administration & Leadership*, 2012:40(2), pp. 248–271.

Bowling, J. C., *Grace-Full Leadership: Understanding The Heart of a Christian Leader*, Beacon Hill Press, Kansas City, 2011.

Cooper, R. & Sawaf, A., *Executive EQ: Emotional Intelligence in Business*, Orion Publishing, London, 1997.

Covey, S. R., *The 7 Habits of Highly Effective People: Powerful Lessons in Personal Change*, Fireside, New York, 1990.

Dewey, J., *How We Think: A Restatement of the Relation of Reflective Thinking to the Educative Process*, D. C. Heath & Co., Boston, 1933.

Dreher, D., *The Tao of Personal Leadership: The Ancient Way to Success*, Thorsons, London, 1997.

Fullan, M., *What's Worth Fighting For? Working Together for Your School*, Ontario Public School Teachers' Federation, Toronto, 1988, pp. 32–36.

Gardner, J. W., *On Leadership*, Free Press, New York, 1990.

Goleman, D., *Working with Emotional Intelligence*, Bloomsbury, London, 1997.

Greenfield, T. & Ribbins, P., *Greenfield on Educational Administration: Towards a Humane Science*, Routledge, London and New York, 1993.

Greenleaf, R. K., *Servant Leadership: A Journey into the Nature of Legitimate Power and Greatness*, Paulist Press, Mahwah, New Jersey, 1977.

Greenleaf, R. K., (eds. D. M. Frick and L. C. Spears), *On Becoming a Servant Leader: The Private Writings of Robert K. Greenleaf*, Jossey-Bass, San Francisco, 1996.

Killion, J. P. & Todnem, G. R., 'A Process for Personal Theory Building,' *Educational Leadership*, 1991:48(6), pp. 14–16.

Larimer, L. V., 'Reflections on Ethics and Integrity,' *HR Focus*, 1997:74, p. 5.

Lucia, A., 'Leaders Know How to Listen,' *HR Focus*, 1997:74, p. 25.

McGahey, V. T., 'Decisional Processes in the Establishment of a Specialist Music School,' unpublished Masters dissertation, Edith Cowan University, Perth, Western Australia, 1993.

McGahey, V. T., 'The Most Important Learners In Schools Are Not The Students!,' *REFLECT Journal*, 1997:3(1), pp. 6–13.

McGahey, V. T., 'Establishing Moral Community in Schools: Sensing the Spirit – A Reflective Discourse in Developing an Ethnographic Study and the Subsequent Analysis of Data,' paper presented at the Annual Conference for Doctorate Students, University of Western Sydney, Sydney, Australia, 2000.

McGahey, V. T., 'School Leadership for Establishing a Moral Community: The Shepherd Metaphor,' *Leading and Managing Journal*, 2000:6(1), pp. 77–94.

McGahey, V. T., 'Establishing Moral Community: Sensing the Spirit,' unpublished doctoral dissertation, University of Western Sydney, Sydney, Australia, 2001.

McGahey, V. T., 'Establishing Moral Community in Schools: Sensing the Spirit of School Leadership,' *Leading and Managing Journal*, 2002:8(1), pp. 60–77.

Roper, D., 'The Lord is My Shepherd: Rest & Renewal from Psalm 23,' 1995. (Available from Our Daily Bread Ministries at www.ourdailybread.org). Retrieved 10 November 1999, from http://www2.gospel com.net/roc/ds/hp952/html/

Schön, D. A., *The Reflective Practitioner: How Professionals Think in Action*, Jossey-Bass, San Francisco, 1983.

Schön, D. A., 'Leadership as Reflection-in-Action,' in Sergiovanni, T. J., *Moral Leadership: Getting to the Heart of School Improvement*, Jossey-Bass, San Francisco, 1992.

Sergiovanni, T. J., *Building Community in Schools*, Jossey-Bass, San Francisco, 1994.

Sergiovanni, T. J., *Leadership for the Schoolhouse: How Is It Different? Why Is It Important?*, Jossey-Bass, San Francisco, 1996.

Shelton, C., 'How to Use Intuition to Build a Whole-Brained Organisation,' *Women in Higher Education*, 1997:6(8), p. 7.

Spears, L. C. (Ed.), *Reflections on Leadership: How Robert K. Greenleaf's Theory of Servant-Leadership Influenced Today's Top Management Thinkers*, John Wiley & Sons, Inc., New York, 1995, pp. 1–14.

Starratt, R. J., *The Drama of Leadership*, Falmer Press, London, 1993.

Starratt, R. J., *Transforming Life in Schools*, Australian Council for Educational Administration, Melbourne, 1993.

Starratt, R. J., *Building an Ethical School: A Practical Response to the Moral Crisis in Schools*, Falmer Press, London, 1994.

Starratt, R. J., *Transforming Educational Administration: Meaning, Community, and Excellence*, McGraw-Hill, New York, 1996.

Vines, H., 'The Core of Good Business,' *HR Monthly*, 1999:6(6), pp. 17–19.

Wagmeister, J. & Shifrin, B., 'Thinking Differently, Learning Differently,' *Educational Leadership*, 2000:58(3), pp. 45–48.

Wenniger, M., 'Learning to Lead with Soul,' *Women in Higher Education*, 1997:6(7), p. 8.

Wenniger, M., 'Why a President Adopts the Servant Leadership Philosophy,' *Women in Higher Education,* 1997:6(8), pp. 1–2.

Westerhof, C., 'Let Intuition Guide your Decision Making on Campus,' *Women in Higher Education*, 1997:6(19), p. 27.

Appendix B

The Conceptual Theories of the Leadership Attributes Study

There are three conceptual theories that underpin the development of the Leadership Attributes. These are the interrelated concepts of learning, leadership and community. Figure 1 displays the link between the three theories. All three concepts are equally significant conceptual theories that form revolving circles of creative reflective thought for the development of the leadership attributes. At the model's centre is the star. This represents the principles, values and beliefs in the formation of the leadership attributes. This model provides the framework for research and the development of Leadership Attributes.

Figure 1. Three Conceptual Theories

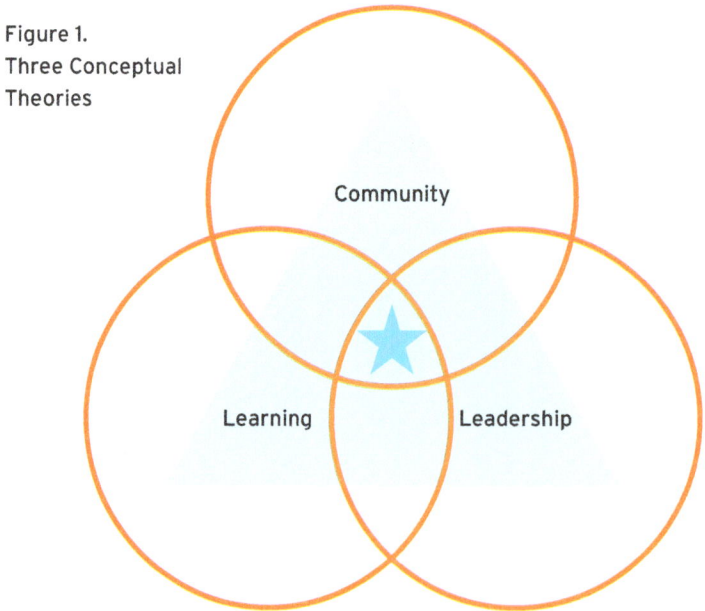

The Structure Explained

The strongest geometrical shape is the triangle. If you wish to build a structure of strength it should have diagonals forming within squares. Thus triangles are formed. Each new diagonal – and, therefore, triangle – builds strength. The circle is a symbol of continuity, eternity and infinity. The cycles of nature, life (carbon dioxide, nitrogen and water) and those we create through economics and business (property cycles) form part of our everyday existence. The structure of a Venn diagram provides intersections of relevance. So it seemed appropriate to develop a model that had strength, continuity and longevity as its basic framework.

The structure is reminiscent of the 'divine proportion' or 'golden ratio'. This principle is evident in paintings by Leonardo da Vinci and the sculptures of Michelangelo and it lies at the heart of all that is music, architecture, prose and poetry, organised and gracefully balanced around a hidden sense of proportion. Indeed, I have tried to capture that in the diagram.

The three conceptual theories are:

- Learning (transformative).
- Leadership (transformational).
- Community (moral).

1. Learning

Learning needs to transform if it is to have a lasting effect. Facilitating learning that is transformational is seen as a way to help meet the global challenge for unity and human survival (Elias, 1997, p. 3).

The term 'transformative learning' was first coined by Jack Mezirow (1975) through his landmark study of women who participated in consciousness-raising groups that critically appraised their perceived and received assumptions about being a woman. In this study, Mezirow observed the dynamics of transformative learning. Mezirow's (1991, p. 6) concept of transformative learning is expressed by Elias (1997, p. 3) as:

> Transformational learning is the transformation of meaning schemes (specific beliefs about self or the world) and meaning perspectives (comprehensive world view) through reflection on underlying premises, leading to meaning perspectives that are more inclusive, differentiated, permanent and integrated.

The University of Toronto's Transformative Learning Centre has developed a working definition that supports the premise of a moral community:

> Transformative learning involves experiencing a deep, structural shift in basic premises of thought, feelings, and actions. It is a shift of consciousness that dramatically and permanently alters our way of being in the world.
>
> This shift includes our understanding of ourselves and our self-locations and our relationships with other humans and with the natural world. It also involves our understanding of power relations in interlocking structures of class, race and gender, our body awareness, our visions of alternative approaches to living, and our sense of possibilities for social justice, peace and personal joy.

Transformative learning involves learning to understand the meaning of what values, ideals, feelings, moral decisions and the concepts of freedom, justice, love, labour, autonomy, commitment and democracy mean to the individual who is also part of a group (Boyd, 2009; Elias, 1997; Heddy & Pugh, 2015; Mezirow, 1991; Senge, 1994). As Taylor (1998, p. 6) states:

> Transformative learning attempts to explain how our expectations, framed within cultural assumptions and presuppositions, directly influence the meaning we derive from our experiences.

The findings of the research project, 'Establishing Moral Community: Sensing the Spirit' (McGahey, 2001, 2002), support the concepts surrounding transformative learning. The research engaged participants in dialogue that allowed them to discuss their perceptions on moral community and leadership while sharing personal and professional experiences.

Significant influences on the theory of transformational learning include Paulo Freire (1970), a constructivist theorist, who describes a process by which adults 'achieve a deepening awareness of both the sociocultural reality which shapes their lives and their capacity to transform that reality through action upon it.'

Constructivism is the assumption that meaning exists within ourselves rather than in external forms.

The Jungian theorists, such as D. Boyd and J. Gordon Myer (Elias, 1997), have a similar view on transformative learning. However, the emphasis is on the self and a process called discernment. Discernment is defined by Elias (1997, p. 4) as 'a process that engages the affective, intuitive and extra-rational resources of the mind.'

For the individual, transformative learning involves becoming more reflective and critical, being more open to the perceptions of others, and being less defensive and more accepting of new ideas (Elias, 1997; Taylor, 1998). Catalysts for transformative learning are disorienting dilemmas and situations that do not fit one's preconceived notions. These dilemmas prompt critical reflection, discernment and the development of new ways of interpreting experiences. In this way, according to Elias (1997, p. 4), 'transformative learning involves reflectively transforming the beliefs, attitudes, opinions, and emotional reactions that constitute our meaning schemes.'

Mezirow (1991, p. 201) believes that transformative educators may help others, and perhaps themselves, move towards a fuller and more dependable understanding of the meaning of our mutual experience. This can be achieved through what Elias (1997, p. 4) terms 'emancipatory discourse'. Such discourse/dialogue happens within a learning community when all participants are aware of the issues, are critically reflective and free to participate (Senge, 1994).

Transformative educators and leaders work with a community to create an environment that will enhance the three critical dimensions of transformative learning. These are given by Elias (1997, p. 4) as:

1. Interpersonal context
   This provides effective support and ensures that all participants have equal access to information exchange.
2. Personal capacities
   This focuses on self-awareness, discernment and inner dialogue, and critical reflection.
3. Flexibility
   Found within individuals and the group to approach some learning appreciatively, some critically, as well as the wisdom to know one from the other.

Recent research on transformative learning supports the earlier studies and writings (Brock, 2015; Courtenay, Merriam et al, 2000; King, 2000; Marcus, McNulty, Dorn & Goralnick, 2014, as cited in Brock, 2015).

2. Leadership

The second conceptual theory is leadership. It has evolved through transformative learning and is traditionally termed transformational leadership. Transformational leadership is the perspective that emanates from transformative learning. There are numerous studies that support the positive relationship between leadership and the learning environment and climate (Vera & Crossan, 2004; Yukl & Lepsinger, 2005).

> Leaders are truly transformational when they increase awareness of what is right, good, important, and beautiful, when they help to elevate followers' needs for achievement and self-actualization, when they foster in followers high moral maturity, and when they move followers to go beyond their self-interests for the good of their group, organization or society. (Bass, 1997, p. 3)

Within the transformational leadership perspective, the leader manages meaning, creates vision and empowers others towards becoming 'self leaders'. This perspective assumes leadership potential in everyone. Sarros, Cooper & Santora (2008) found that articulating a vision and providing support helped to build a climate for innovation and creativity within the workplace. In such a workplace environment, a study also revealed that ambidexterity was enhanced (Nemanich & Vera, 2009). In this context, ambidexterity is the 'ability to explore new capabilities while exploiting existing ones' (Hetland et al, 2011). This is also supported by Ramdorai & Herstatt (2015) in the book *Frugal Innovation in Healthcare: How Targeting Low-Income Markets Leads to Disruptive Innovation*.

Therefore, from this perspective, leadership is seen as communal – it relies on the collective voice of a community that is constantly engaging in dialogue within itself and with the greater world. This style of leadership encourages the 'honest' sharing of thoughts and ideas and, in this sense, can be seen to be less domineering. People are empowered when they perceive the leadership is transformational (Hetland et al, 2011).

For as Starratt (1993, p. 8) states, transformational leaders 'encourage followers to function collectively at a higher moral level, transcending their more self-serving motives for the achievement of some higher common good.'

This moral nature of transformative leadership is shared by Bass (1997) and Burns (1978, 1984). Further to this, Burns (1984, p. 7) spoke of transformational leadership as a quest for personal growth through transformation:

> Transforming leadership carries grave but always recognized moral implications ... [The result of such leadership is to raise] ... the level of human conduct and ethical aspirations of both leader and led, and thus it has a transforming effect on both [transformative learning has occurred].

Burns saw transformation as one that was necessarily elevating, furthering what was good rather than evil for the person and the polity. Therefore, Burns (1978, p. 21) did not regard someone like Hitler as being a transformational leader for even though:

Germany was still transformed, the leadership itself was immoral, brutal, and extremely costly in life, liberty, property, and the pursuit of happiness to his victims, and in the long run, to his 'Master Race'.

Bass, back in 1985, did not agree with Burns. Bass (1985) argued that Hitler's leadership was transformational, even though it might be depicted as having evil purposes rather than morally elevating ones. However, Bass has since had a change of heart and introduced a new term 'authentic transformational leadership'. Bass (1997, p. 2) states that:

> In agreement with Burns, we [Bass and Associates] argue here that authentic transformational leadership must be grounded in moral foundations. The ethics of leadership rest upon three pillars:
>
> 1. The moral character of the leader.
> 2. The ethical values embedded in the leader's vision, articulation, and program which followers either embrace or reject.
> 3. The morality of the processes of social ethical choice and action that leaders and followers engage in and collectively pursue.

Such ethical dimensions of leadership have been widely acknowledged (Greenleaf, 1977; Kouzes & Posner, 2007; Wren, 1998). Transformational leaders set examples to be emulated by their followers. When leaders are more morally mature, those they lead display higher moral reasoning (Burns, 1978; Dukerich, Nichols et al, 1990). From this perspective, a community can begin a transformation into a more moral community.

3. Community

> The challenge of building a richer form of community in our schools is a reflection of the challenges facing our society at large, namely, the widespread creation of richer forms of community life. (Starratt, 1996, p. 93)

The onslaught of globalisation (an effort towards making the world as one unified community) has been instrumental in causing the need for people to develop tolerance, the ability to accept diversity and, at the very least, to accept change. Such willingness to listen and value the human rights of others is the essence of a moral community. A moral community is sought rather than an 'ordinary' community, because the 'ideal' of a moral community is to listen to all voices and, in particular, the voice within oneself (transformative learning concept). From this listening, a community can extrapolate, formulate, and start to live out shared ideals and create a shared vision.

The concept of moral community echoes the angelic tones of a sacred ideal – a higher level of community growth and achievement. Theorists and researchers have written about community and moral community (Barth, 1990; Dreher, 1997; Etzioni in Berreth & Scherer, 1993; Etzioni, 1993; McGahey, 2001; Sergiovanni, 1992, 1994; Shivers, 1994; Starratt, 1996).

In his studies on moral community, Sergiovanni (1996, p. 48) believes communities are 'collections of individuals who are bonded together by natural will and who are together bound to a set of shared ideas and ideals.' This view is shared with Starratt (1996, p. 87), who writes 'communities tend to signify a group of equals who are bonded together in friendship and shared values.'

More recently, writers in the field speak of community that is moral when members have rights, privileges and duties towards other community members (Hudson, 2015; Stephens, 2015).

A study – 'Establishing Moral Community: Sensing the Spirit' (McGahey, 2001, 2002) – explored the beliefs and philosophies of school leaders in the formation of moral community within the context of a Catholic school. They defined moral community as:

> … a community that values the heart, soul and mind of its people through the growth and development of shared principles, values and beliefs.

A moral community is found through the sharing of principles, values, beliefs, and the open and honest dialogue with all members of a community. Leaders play a key role in this dialogue by ensuring that all voices are heard.

In his work on an ethical school community, Starratt (1994, p. 136) believes the following qualities are paramount in striving to build an ethical (moral) community:

> … great courage, a modicum of intelligence, lots of humility, humour and compassion, and an unyielding hope in the endurance and heroism of human beings. It is a dream worthy of educators.

Bibliography

Barth, R. S., *Improving Schools from Within: Teachers, Parents, and Principals can Make the Difference*, Jossey-Bass, San Francisco, 1990.

Bass, B. M., *Leadership and Performance Beyond Expectations*, Free Press, New York, 1985.

Bass, B. M., 'The Ethics of Transformative Leadership,' in *KLSP Transformational Leadership: Working Papers*, Academy of Leadership Press, University of Maryland, Maryland, 1997. Retrieved 17 April 2001, from http://www.academy.umd.edu/scholarship/caslklspdocs/bbass_pl.htm. Available at http://www.sciencedirect.com/science/article/pii/S1048984399000168.

Berreth, D. & Scherer, M., 'On Transmitting Values: A Conversation with Amitai Etzioni,' *Educational Leadership*, 1993:51(3), pp. 12–15.

Boyd, B. L., 'Using a Case Study to Develop the Transformational Teaching Theory,' *Journal of Leadership Education*, 2009:7(3), pp. 50–59.

Brock, S., 'Let's Spread the Word About the Wisdom of Transformative Learning,' *Journal of Transformative Learning*, 2015:3(1), pp. 18–21.

Bryk, A. S., Lee, V. E. & Holland, P. B., *Catholic Schools and the Common Good*, Harvard University Press, Cambridge, Massachusetts, 1993.

Burns, J. M., *Leadership*, Harper & Row, New York, 1978.

Burns, J. M., Foreword, in Kellerman, B. (Ed.) *Leadership: Multidisciplinary Perspectives*, Prentice-Hall, Englewood Cliffs, New Jersey, 1984.

Courtenay, B. C., Merriam, S., Reeves, P. & Baumgartner, L., 'Perspective Transformation over Time: A 2-Year Follow-up Study of HIV-Positive Adults,' *Adult Education Quarterly*, 2000:50(2), pp. 102–119.

Dreher, D., *The Tao of Personal Leadership: The Ancient Way to Success*, Thorsons, London, 1997.

Dukerich, J. M., Nichols, M. L., Elm, D. R. & Vollrath, D. A., 'Moral Reasoning in Groups: Leaders Make a Difference,' *Human Relations*, 1990:43, pp. 473–493.

Elias, D., 'It's Time to Change our Minds: An Introduction to Transformative Learning,' *ReVision*, 1997:20(1), pp. 2–6.

Etzioni, A., *The Spirit of Community: Rights, Responsibilities and the Communitarian Agenda*, Crown Publishers Inc., New York, 1993.

Freire, P., *Pedagogy of the Oppressed*, Continuum, New York, 1970.

Greenleaf, R. K., *Servant Leadership: A Journey into the Nature of Legitimate Power and Greatness*, Paulist Press, Mahwah, New Jersey, 1977.

Heddy, B. & Pugh, K., 'Bigger is Not Always Better: Should Educators Aim for Big Transformative Learning Events or Small Transformative Experiences?,' *Journal of Transformative Learning*, 2015:3(1), pp. 52–58.

Hemenway, P., *The Secret Code: The Mysterious Formula that Rules Art, Nature, and Science*, Evergreen, Cologne, Germany, 2008.

Hetland, H., Skogstad, A., Hetland, J. & Mikkelsen, A., 'Leadership and Learning Climate in a Work Setting,' *European Psychologist*, 2011:16(3), pp. 163–173.

Hudson, B., 'Moral Communities Across the Border: the Particularism of Law Meets the Universalism of Ethics,' in Webber, L. (Ed) *Rethinking Border Control for a Globalizing World: A Preferred Future*, Routledge, Abingdon, Oxfordshire and New York, 2015, p. 116.

King, K. P., 'The Adult ESL Experience: Facilitating Perspective Transformation in the Classroom,' *Adult Basic Education*, 2000:10(2), p. 69.

Kouzes, J. M. & Posner, B. Z., *The Leadership Challenge*, Jossey-Bass, San Francisco, 2007.

McGahey, V. T., 'Establishing Moral Community in Schools: Sensing the Spirit,' unpublished log/diary entries, University of Western Sydney, Sydney, Australia, 2001.

McGahey, V. T., 'Establishing Moral Community in Schools: Sensing the Spirit of School Leadership,' *Leading and Managing Journal*, 2002:8(1), pp. 60–77.

Marcus, L. J., McNulty, E., Dorn, B. C. & Goralnick, E., 'Crisis Meta-Leadership Lessons from the Boston Marathon Bombings Response,' 2014, in Brock, S., 'Let's Spread the Word About the Wisdom of Transformative Learning,' *Journal of Transformative Learning*, 2015:3(1), pp. 18–21.

Mezirow. J., *Transformative Dimensions of Adult Learning*, Jossey-Bass, San Francisco, 1991.

Nemanich, L. A. & Vera, D., 'Transformational Leadership and Ambidexterity in the Context of an Acquisition,' *The Leadership Quarterly*, 2009:20(1), pp. 19–33.

Ramdorai, A. & Herstatt, C., *Frugal Innovation in Healthcare: How Targeting Low-Income Markets Leads to Disruptive Innovation*, Springer International Publishing, Switzerland, 2015, pp. 105–130.

Sarros, J. C., Cooper, B. K. & Santora, J. C., 'Building a Climate for Innovation through Transformational Leadership and Organizational Culture,' *Journal of Leadership & Organizational Studies*, 2008:15(2), pp. 145–158, p. 145.

Senge, P. M., *The Fifth Discipline: The Art & Practice of The Learning Organization*, Currency Doubleday, New York, 1990.

Sergiovanni, T. J., *Moral Leadership: Getting to the Heart of School Improvement*, Jossey-Bass, San Francisco, 1992.

Sergiovanni, T. J., *Building Community in Schools*, Jossey-Bass, San Francisco, 1994.

Sergiovanni, T. J., *Leadership for the Schoolhouse: How Is It Different? Why Is It Important?*, Jossey-Bass, San Francisco, 1996.

Starratt, R. J., *The Drama of Leadership*, Falmer Press, London, 1993.

Starratt, R. J., *Building an Ethical School: A Practical Response to the Moral Crisis in Schools*, Falmer Press, London, 1994.

Starratt, R. J., *Transforming Educational Administration: Meaning, Community, and Excellence*, McGraw-Hill, New York, 1996.

Stephens, C., 'The Moral Community And Moral Consideration: A Pragmatic Approach,' unpublished thesis, 2015. (Available at: http://hdl.handle.net/10019.1/97136)

Taylor, E. W., 'The Theory and Practice of Transformative Learning: A Critical Review,' ERIC Clearinghouse, 1998. Retrieved 4 March 2001 at http:///www.nifl.gov/nifl-family/1998/0400.html. (Available at http://files.eric.ed.gov/fulltext/ED423422.pdf)

The Transformative Learning Centre, Ontario Institute for Studies in Education, University of Toronto: http://tlc.oise.utoronto.ca/About.html

Vera, D. & Crossan, M., 'Strategic Leadership and Organizational Learning,' *Academy of Management Review*, 2004:29(2), pp. 222–240.

Wren, J. T., 'James Madison and the Ethics of Transformational Leadership,' 1998, in Ciulla, J. B. (Ed.), *Ethics, the Heart of Leadership*, Praeger, Westport, Connecticut, 1998, pp. 145–168.

Yukl, G. & Lepsinger, R., 'Why Integrating the Leading and Managing Roles is Essential for Organizational Effectiveness,' *Organizational Dynamics*, 2005:34(4), pp. 361–375.

Appendix C

The Shepherd Metaphor

This appendix presents a simplistic and summarised version of 'The Shepherd Metaphor' of leadership. As you read the book, you will see how the Leadership Attributes (Chapters 3–9) and the Leadership Attributes in Action (Chapter 10) fit into the model. You will notice how it has been developed further since its inception in the late 1990s. An older, yet more detailed, version of the model is given in published articles (McGahey, 2000[a], 2002) and thesis document (McGahey, 2001).

Through my work in the field of leadership, I developed the Shepherd Leadership Model that I live by. I have continually refined the model and developed several other breakaway concepts that are used to describe significant aspects of the model. The model consists of a guiding principle, leadership attributes, values and actions, which are things held to be true.

The Shepherd Metaphor: Sensing the Spirit

> It is not more light that is needed in the world,
> it is more warmth.
> We will not die of darkness but of cold.
>
> **Jenny Read**

The essence of leadership is poignantly expressed in this quote by sculptor Jenny Read in Cooper & Sawaf (1997, p. 215). It is leadership that shines like a beacon to attract people, but also keeps people together through the sheer warmth emanating from the source – the warmth is what will draw people towards the leader. This warmth is expressed through qualities such as empathy and compassion. These attributes

Leadership Attributes for Women and Men

The Shepherd Metaphor
Sensing the spirit

Guiding Principle: *Life is the precious gift*

Shepherd Attributes

Integrity
Trust and Trustworthy

Prophecy
Transcendence and Faith

Empathy
Compassion and Passion

Intuition
Risk

Judgment
Diversity

Communication
Consistency

Shepherd Values

Respect

Truth

Authenticity

Resilience

Tolerance

Ingenuity

Wisdom

Shepherd Actions

Gathering
Vision and mission

Presence
Always there

Pathfinding
Guide for the journey

arise from the principles and values that profoundly influence human thoughts and deeds (Covey, 1994; Goleman, 1997; McGahey, 1997; Sergiovanni, 1992, 1994; Starratt, 1994). Covey (1994, p. 35) believes there is a clear distinction between a principle and a value:

> Principles are not values. A gang of thieves can share values, but they are in violation of the fundamental principles we are talking about. Principles are the territory. Values are the maps. When we value correct principles, we have truth – a knowledge of things as they are.

Within the model there is only one principle: Life is the precious gift. The important word here is 'life'. It is life that is the gift – each breath we take. The gift is not all the trappings, such as material possessions. Just being alive and living is the gift. 'Life is the precious gift' is the foundation upon which the model rests. There is no better story than the biblical parable of The Lost Sheep (Luke 15: 3–6). The shepherd leaves the 99 sheep to go and search for the one lost sheep. He knew the flock could look after itself while he ventured out to find the lost one. The importance of the individual above the needs of the collective resonates here. The parables of the Prodigal Son (Luke 15: 11–32) and the Good Samaritan (Luke 10: 30–37) also follow this theme.

Several human values and likely behaviours reflect this principle. These are largely derived from the work of several writers, including Bezzina (2012), Covey (1994), Dreher (1997), Fullan (1988), McGahey (1993), Sergiovanni (1992, 1994) and Wenniger (1997). Most of these values have been iterated in the works of Greenleaf (1977) and others who speak of servant leadership (Gardner, 1990; Shelton, 1997; Spears, 1995; Starratt, 2005, 2012). The following list is by no means inclusive of all possible values, but most can be linked to those listed below. Attached to each value is a brief description of the meaning behind the value:

- Respect – for human life and the dignity of all people.
- Truth – seek the truth … without truth there is no trust and no hope.

- Authenticity – what you see is what you get.
- Resilience – acknowledge the situation without allowing it to destroy you within.
- Tolerance – an acceptance of the things you can change and those you cannot.
- Ingenuity – make something out of nothing; seek to create.
- Wisdom – listen to the voice within … this voice is your best teacher to create a future filled with goodness.

Each of the values can be fostered in practices that reflect the attributes and actions of a leader as given in The Shepherd Metaphor. In this way, authentic relationships of trust are built and nurtured. As previously stated, several writers in the field of leadership have realised the significance of relationships (personal and group) in organisations and the formation of communities (Bezzina, 2012; Bowling, 2011; McGahey, 2000[b]; Sergiovanni, 1996; Starratt, 2012).

From these values, several attributes can be found that give purpose to the shepherd leader's role. These attributes are considered essential for the shepherd leader within the context of a moral community – a community in which all members endeavour to live as shepherd leaders who lead with grace.

The shepherd attributes, founded through a shared principle and shared values and beliefs, should emerge from within the hearts, souls and minds of all the members of a moral community. The shepherd actions can then evolve through the active participation of the community to live out a shared graceful vision for a grace-filled mission. Therefore, a community should not need to overreact to challenge and change. As Bowling (2011, p. 41) states 'change is not the enemy; changing the wrong things is. It takes grace to know the difference.'

There are three strategic action components to The Shepherd Metaphor of leadership. These are:

- Gathering – Vision and mission.
- Pathfinding – Guide for the journey.
- Presence – Always there.

Gathering is essential to secure followership. You're not a leader without followers. Therefore, it relies on the leader's vision and mission to draw followers to the leader. Leadership within followership; followership through leadership.

Once gathered, it is essential that the leader's vision and mission point towards an achievable path and become a shared vision and mission.

Finally, the team and community need to always feel the leader's presence – that he or she will always be there.

A shepherd-led community would realise that their security is not based on external sources but on an inward principle and associated values and attributes that form a foundation stone for a graceful vision for a grace-filled mission that is a call to action in the service of others – where the actions seem effortless, paradoxical and defying all logic because:

> The best runner leaves no tracks …
> The best door needs nothing to secure it.
> The best knot does not bind,
> Yet cannot be loosened. (Tao, 27)
> **(Dreher, 1997, p. 257)**

So our task as shepherd leaders is simple – be still and watch; remain mindful and filled with hope, but still willing to make a decision when needed. Indeed, this is grace in its purest form – a graceful vision for a grace-filled mission is a call to action.

Conclusion

Simplistic by design, the concept of The Shepherd Metaphor touches at the soul of what it is to lead and be called a leader. The Shepherd Metaphor is not associated with a set of skills or managerial tasks that can be taught. Indeed, the guiding principle, the leadership attributes and the leadership actions need to be found, developed within and then lived through action – and, not just by those in leadership or who seek leadership roles. The Shepherd Metaphor is a metaphor for living a good life. But the teachings of the metaphor must first be desired, then sought, found, and lived in our daily life with each breath we take.

The Shepherd Metaphor can be used by leader(s) to guide them in their daily work within community. It strikes at the heart of what is essentially human and humane – a life that is served and a life that gives service; a life of contemplative reflection translated into vision, mission and action; and a path of hope.

Bibliography

Bezzina, M., 'Paying Attention to Moral Purpose in Leading Learning: Lessons from the Leaders Transforming Learning and Learners Project,' *Educational Management Administration & Leadership*, 2012:40(2), pp. 248–271.

Bowling, J. C., *Grace-Full Leadership: Understanding The Heart of a Christian Leader*, Beacon Hill Press, Kansas City, 2011.

Cooper, R. & Sawaf, A., *Executive EQ: Emotional Intelligence in Business*, Orion Publishing, London, 1997.

Covey, S. R., *The 7 Habits of Highly Effective People: Powerful Lessons in Personal Change*, Simon & Schuster, New York, 1994.

Dreher, D., *The Tao of Personal Leadership: The Ancient Way to Success*, Thorsons, London, 1997.

Fullan, M., *What's Worth Fighting For? Working Together for Your School*, Ontario Public School Teachers' Federation, Toronto, 1988, pp. 32–36.

Gardner, J. W., *On Leadership*, Free Press, New York, 1990.

Goleman, D., *Working with Emotional Intelligence*, Bloomsbury, London, 1997.

Greenleaf, R. K., *Servant Leadership: A Journey into the Nature of Legitimate Power and Greatness*, Paulist Press, Mahwah, New Jersey, 1977.

McGahey, V. T., 'Decisional Processes in the Establishment of a Specialist Music School,' unpublished Masters dissertation, Edith Cowan University, Perth, Western Australia, 1993.

McGahey, V. T., 'The Most Important Learners In Schools Are Not The Students!,' *REFLECT Journal*, 1997:3(1), pp. 6–13.

McGahey, V. T., 'Establishing Moral Community in Schools: Sensing the Spirit – A Reflective Discourse in Developing an Ethnographic Study and the Subsequent Analysis of Data,' paper presented at the Annual Conference for Doctorate Students, University of Western Sydney, Sydney, Australia, 2000[a].

McGahey, V. T., 'School Leadership for Establishing a Moral Community: The Shepherd Metaphor,' *Leading and Managing Journal*, 2000[b]:6(1), pp. 77–94.

McGahey, V. T., 'Establishing Moral Community in Schools: Sensing the Spirit of School Leadership,' *Leading and Managing Journal*, 2002:8(1), pp. 60–77.

Sergiovanni, T. J., *Moral Leadership: Getting to the Heart of School Improvement*, Jossey-Bass, San Francisco, 1992.

Sergiovanni, T. J., *Building Community in Schools*, Jossey-Bass, San Francisco, 1994.

Sergiovanni, T. J., *Leadership for the Schoolhouse: How Is It Different? Why Is It Important?*, Jossey-Bass, San Francisco, 1996.

Shelton, C., 'How to Use Intuition to Build a Whole-Brained Organisation,' *Women in Higher Education*, 1997:6(8), p. 7.

Spears, L. C. (Ed.), *Reflections on Leadership: How Robert K. Greenleaf's Theory of Servant-Leadership Influenced Today's Top Management Thinkers*, John Wiley & Sons, Inc., New York, 1995, pp. 1–14.

Starratt, R. J., *Building an Ethical School: A Practical Response to the Moral Crisis in Schools*, Falmer Press, London, 1994.

Starratt, R. J., 'Cultivating The Moral Character Of Learning And Teaching: A Neglected Dimension Of Educational Leadership,' *School Leadership And Management*, 2005:25(4), pp. 399–411.

Starratt, R. J., *Cultivating An Ethical School*, Routledge, New York, 2012.

Wenniger, M., 'Learning to Lead with Soul,' *Women in Higher Education*, 1997:6(7), p. 8.

Appendix D
The Invitation

It doesn't interest me
what you do for a living.
I want to know
what you ache for
and if you dare to dream
of meeting your heart's longing.

It doesn't interest me
how old you are.
I want to know
if you will risk
looking like a fool
for love
for your dream
for the adventure of being alive.

It doesn't interest me
what planets are
squaring your moon ...
I want to know
if you have touched
the centre of your own sorrow
if you have been opened
by life's betrayals
or have become shrivelled and closed
from fear of further pain.

I want to know
if you can sit with pain
mine or your own
without moving to hide it
or fade it
or fix it.

The Invitation

I want to know
if you can be with joy
mine or your own
if you can dance with wildness
and let the ecstasy fill you
to the tips of your fingers and toes
without cautioning us
to be careful
to be realistic
to remember the limitations
of being human.

It doesn't interest me
if the story you are telling me
is true.
I want to know if you can
disappoint another
to be true to yourself.
If you can bear
the accusation of betrayal
and not betray your own soul.
If you can be faithless
and therefore trustworthy.

I want to know
if you can see Beauty
even when it is not pretty
every day.
And if you can source your own life
from its presence.

I want to know
if you can live with failure
yours and mine
and still stand at the edge of the lake
and shout to the silver of the full moon,
'Yes.'

Leadership Attributes for Women and Men

It doesn't interest me
to know where you live
or how much money you have.
I want to know if you can get up
after the night of grief and despair
weary and bruised to the bone
and do what needs to be done
to feed the children.

It doesn't interest me
who you know
or how you came to be here.
I want to know if you will stand
in the centre of the fire
with me
and not shrink back.

It doesn't interest me
where or what or with whom
you have studied.
I want to know
what sustains you
from the inside
when all else falls away.

I want to know
if you can be alone
with yourself
and if you truly like
the company you keep
in the empty moments.

By Oriah Mountain Dreamer from her book, THE INVITATION © 1999.
Published by HarperONE, San Francisco. All rights reserved.
Presented with permission of the author. www.oriah.org

Appendix E

Benjamin Franklin's 13 Virtues

Temperance: Eat not to dullness; drink not to elevation.

Silence: Speak not but what may benefit others or yourself; avoid trifling conversation.

Order: Let all your things have their places; let each part of your business have its time.

Resolution: Resolve to perform what you ought; perform without fail what you resolve.

Frugality: Make no expense but to do good to others or yourself; i.e., waste nothing.

Industry: Lose no time; be always employed in something useful; cut off all unnecessary actions.

Sincerity: Use no hurtful deceit; think innocently and justly; and, if you speak, speak accordingly.

Justice: Wrong none by doing injuries, or omitting the benefits that are your duty.

Moderation: Avoid extremes; forbear resenting injuries so much as you think they deserve.

Cleanliness: Tolerate no uncleanliness in body, clothes, or habitation.

Tranquillity: Be not disturbed at trifles, or at accidents common or unavoidable.

Chastity: Rarely use venery but for health or offspring, never to dullness, weakness, or the injury of your own or another's peace or reputation.

Humility: Imitate Jesus and Socrates.

Source: http://www.virtuesforlife.com/benjamin-franklin-on-living-a-virtuous-life/

Endnotes

Introduction

1. Lowry, H. (Producer) & Zucker, J. (Director), *First Knight* [movie], Columbia TriStar, Los Angeles, 1995.
2. McGahey, V. T., 'Establishing Moral Community: Sensing the Spirit,' unpublished doctoral dissertation, University of Western Sydney, Sydney, Australia, 2001
3. McGahey, V. T., 'Establishing Moral Community: Sensing the Spirit.'
4. McGahey, V. T., 'Establishing Moral Community: Sensing the Spirit'; McGahey, V. T., 'Establishing Moral Community in Schools: Sensing the Spirit of School Leadership,' *Leading and Managing Journal*, 2002:8(1), pp. 60–77; McGahey, V. T., 'School Leadership for Establishing a Moral Community: The Shepherd Metaphor,' *Leading and Managing Journal*, 2000:6(1), pp. 77–94.

Chapter 1

1. Kane, S. & Kane, L., *The Little Brown Book: Mary MacKillop's Spirituality in our Everyday Lives*, St Pauls Publications, Strathfield, Australia, 2011.
2. Daft, R. L., *The Leadership Experience*, Cengage Learning, Stamford, Connecticut, 2015.
3. McGahey, V. T., 'School Leadership for Establishing a Moral Community: The Shepherd Metaphor,' *Leading and Managing Journal*, 2000:6(1), p. 77; McGahey, V. T., 'Establishing Moral Community in Schools: Sensing the Spirit of School Leadership,' *Leading and Managing Journal*, 2002:8(1), pp. 60–77; Copeland, M. K., 'The Emerging Significance of Values Based Leadership: A Literature Review,' *International Journal of Leadership Studies*, 2014:8(2), 105, p. 131.
4. McGahey, V. T., 'Establishing Moral Community in Schools: Sensing the Spirit of School Leadership,' pp. 60–77.
5. Available at http://www.un.org/en/documents/udhr/
6. Ramdorai, A. & Herstatt, C., *Frugal Innovation in Healthcare: How Targeting Low-Income Markets Leads to Disruptive Innovation*, Springer International Publishing, Switzerland, 2015; Sandström, C., Berglund, H. & Magnusson, M., 'Symmetric Assumptions in the Theory of Disruptive Innovation – Theoretical and Managerial Implications,' *Creativity and Management*, Vol. 23(4), pp. 472–483; Yamagata-Lynch, L. C., Cowan, J. & Luetkehans, L. M., 'Transforming Disruptive Technology into Sustainable Technology: Understanding the Front-End Design of an Online Program at a Brick-and-Mortar University,' *The Internet and Higher Education*, Vol. 26, July 2015, pp. 10-18.
7. By Oriah Mountain Dreamer from her book, THE INVITATION © 1999. Published by HarperONE, San Francisco. All rights reserved. Presented with permission of the author. www.oriah.org
8. Available at http://www.ceda.com.au/research-and-policy/research/2013/06/6/wil2013
9. Kellerman, B., *Followership: How Followers are Creating Change and Changing Leaders*, Recording for the Blind & Dyslexic, Harvard Business Press, Princeton, New Jersey, 2008.
10. McGahey, V. T., 'School Leadership for Establishing A Moral Community: The Shepherd Metaphor.'

Endnotes

Chapter 2

1. This is a modified version of several that can be found on the internet.
2. Kerner, J. (Producer) & Gosnell, R. (Director), *The Smurfs* [movie], Columbia Pictures, Los Angeles, 2011.
3. Queen Elizabeth II, Diamond Jubilee speech to Parliament, 2012. (Retrieved from http://speakingfrog.com/?p=1075)
4. Robinson, M., The 2009 Griffith Lecture with Mary Robinson, Radio National: Big Ideas, 2009. (Retrieved from http://www.abc.net.au/radionational/programs/bigideas/the-2009-griffith-lecture-with-mary-robinson/3099570)
5. Bennis, W., 'The Art of Leading Well,' HBR IdeaCast, 29 July 2010. Available at https://hbr.org/2010/07/the-art-of-leading-well
6. Bezzina, M., 'Moral Purpose and Shared Leadership: The Leaders Transforming Learning and Learners Pilot Study,' 2007–The Leadership Challenge–Improving Learning in Schools, available at http://research.acer.edu.au/research_conference_2007/14; McGahey, V. T., 'Establishing Moral Community in Schools: Sensing the Spirit of School Leadership,' *Leading and Managing Journal*, 2002:8(1), pp. 60-77; Starratt, R. J., *Ethical Leadership*, Jossey-Bass, San Francisco, 2005, pp. 61–74.
7. Bezzina, M., Paying Attention to Moral Purpose in Leading Learning, Lessons from the Leaders Transforming Learning and Learners Project, *Educational Management Administration & Leadership*, 2012:40(2), pp. 248–271; McGahey, V. T., 'Establishing Moral Community in Schools: Sensing the Spirit of School Leadership'; McGahey, V. T., 'School Leadership for Establishing a Moral Community: The Shepherd Metaphor,' *Leading and Managing Journal*, 2000:6(1), pp. 77–94; Sergiovanni, T. J., *Moral Leadership: Getting to the Heart of School Improvement*, Jossey-Bass, San Francisco, 1992; Starratt, R. J., *Cultivating an Ethical School*, Routledge, New York, 2012.
8. Available at http://www.virtuesforlife.com/benjamin-franklin-on-living-a-virtuous-life/
9. Remen, R. N., *Kitchen Table Wisdom: Stories That Heal*, Pan Macmillan Australia, Sydney, Australia, 2002, pp. 88–89.
10. Canfield, J. & Hansen, M. V., *Chicken Soup for the Soul: 101 Stories to Open the Heart & Rekindle the Spirit*, Health Communications, Deerfield Park, Florida, 1993.
11. Bolman, L. G. & Deal, T. E., *Leading with Soul: An Uncommon Journey of Spirit*, Jossey-Bass, San Francisco, 2011; Bowling, J. C., *Grace-Full Leadership: Understanding the Heart of a Christian Leader*, Beacon Hill Press, Kansas City, 2011; Greenfield, T. & Ribbins, P., *Greenfield on Educational Administration: Towards a Humane Science*, Routledge, London and New York, 1993; Shelton, C., 'How to Use Intuition to Build a Whole-Brained Organisation,' *Women in Higher Education*, 1997:6(8), p. 7; McCormick, B. & Davenport, D., *Shepherd Leadership: Wisdom for Leaders from Psalm 23*, Jossey-Bass, San Francisco, 2003; Starratt, R. J., *The Drama of Leadership*, Falmer Press, London, 1993; Starratt, R. J., *Transforming Educational Administration: Meaning, Community, and Excellence*, McGraw-Hill, New York, 1996; Wenniger, M., 'Learning to Lead with Soul,' *Women in Higher Education*, 1997:6(7), p. 8; Westerhof, C., 'Let Intuition Guide your Decision Making on Campus,' *Women in Higher Education*, 1997:6(19), p. 27.
12. Lowney, C., *Heroic Living: Discover Your Purpose and Change the World*, Loyola Press, Chicago, 2009, p. 19.
13. Bredfeldt, G. J., *Great Leader, Great Teacher: Recovering the Biblical Vision for Leadership*, Moody Publishers, Chicago, 2006, p. 153.

14 McCormick, B. & Davenport, D., *Shepherd Leadership: Wisdom for Leaders from Psalm 23*, p. 3.
15 Wenniger, M., 'Learning to Lead with Soul,' p. 8.
16 Bowling, J. C., *Grace-Full Leadership: Understanding the Heart of a Christian Leader*, p. 37; Lowney, C., *Heroic Living: Discover your Purpose and Change the World*, p. 151; McCormick, B. & Davenport, D., *Shepherd Leadership: Wisdom for Leaders from Psalm 23*, p. 25.

Chapter 3

1 Cooper, R. & Sawaf, A., *Executive EQ: Emotional Intelligence in Business*, Orion Publishing, London, 1997, p. 215.
2 McGahey, V. T., 'Establishing Moral Community in Schools: Sensing the Spirit of School Leadership,' *Leading and Managing Journal*, 2002:8(1), pp. 60–77; McGahey, V. T., 'Establishing Moral Community: Sensing the Spirit,' unpublished doctoral dissertation, University of Western Sydney, Sydney, Australia, 2001; McGahey, V. T., 'School Leadership for Establishing a Moral Community: The Shepherd Metaphor,' *Leading and Managing Journal*, 2000:6(1), pp. 77–94; McGahey, V. T., 'Establishing Moral Community in Schools: Sensing the Spirit – A Reflective Discourse in Developing an Ethnographic Study and the Subsequent Analysis of Data,' paper presented at the Annual Conference for Doctorate Students, University of Western Sydney, Sydney, Australia, 2000; McGahey, V. T., 'School Leadership for Building a Moral Community: The Shepherd Metaphor,' paper presented at the ACEA International Conference, Education the Global Challenge: Community Building in a Global Context, Hobart, Australia, 2000.

Chapter 4

1 Available at https://dmihrd.wordpress.com/tag/greatness/
2 Kouzes, J. M. & Posner, B. Z., *Credibility: How Leaders Gain and Lose It, Why People Demand It*, Jossey-Bass, San Francisco, 1993, pp. 12–15, from Dreher, D., *The Tao of Personal Leadership: The Ancient Way to Success*, Thorsons, London, 1997, p. 270.
3 McGahey, V. T., 'Establishing Moral Community in Schools: Sensing the Spirit of School Leadership,' *Leading and Managing Journal*, 2002:8(1), pp. 60–77.
4 McGahey, V. T., 'Establishing Moral Community in Schools: Sensing the Spirit of School Leadership'; McGahey, V. T., 'Establishing Moral Community: Sensing the Spirit,' unpublished doctoral dissertation, University of Western Sydney, Sydney, Australia, 2001.
5 Bezzina, M., Burford, C. & Duignan, P., 'Leaders Transforming Learning and Learners: Messages for Catholic Leaders,' 4th International Conference on Catholic Education Leadership, Sydney, Vol. 29, 2007; McGahey, V. T., 'Establishing Moral Community in Schools: Sensing the Spirit of School Leadership,' 2002; Starratt, R. J., 'Cultivating The Moral Character Of Learning And Teaching: A Neglected Dimension Of Educational Leadership,' *School Leadership And Management*, 2005:25(4), pp. 399–411.
6 Bezzina, M., 'Paying Attention to Moral Purpose in Leading Learning: Lessons from the Leaders Transforming Learning and Learners Project,' *Educational Management Administration & Leadership*, 2012:40(2), pp. 248–271; Bowling, J. C., *Grace-Full Leadership: Understanding the Heart of a Christian Leader*, Beacon Hill Press, Kansas City,

2011; McGahey, V. T., 'School Leadership for Establishing a Moral Community: The Shepherd Metaphor,' *Leading and Managing Journal*, 2000:6(1), pp. 77–94; McGahey, V. T., 'Establishing Moral Community in Schools: Sensing the Spirit of School Leadership'; Sergiovanni, T. J., *Leadership for the Schoolhouse: How Is It Different? Why Is It Important?*, Jossey-Bass, San Francisco, 1996; Starratt, R. J., *Cultivating an Ethical School*, Routledge, New York, 2012.

7   Available at http://www.inspirationalstories.com/1/105.html
8   Lee, B., *The Power Principle: Influence with Honor,* Simon and Schuster, New York, 1998, p. 170. Also available at http://www.spiritual-short-stories.com/spiritual-short-story-87-Ghandi+and+Some+Sugar.html
9   Covey, S. R., *The 7 Habits of Highly Effective People: Powerful Lessons in Personal Change*, Fireside, New York, 1990, p. 178.
10 Available at http://www.citehr.com/89599-trust-small-story-read-big-message.html
11 Available at http://www.inspirationalstories.com/7/709.html
12 McGahey, V. T., 'Establishing Moral Community in Schools: Sensing the Spirit of School Leadership'; McGahey, V. T., 'Establishing Moral Community: Sensing the Spirit.'
13 Available at http://www.businessballs.com/stories.htm
14 Bowling, J. C., *Grace-Full Leadership: Understanding the Heart of a Christian Leader*; Sergiovanni, T. J., *Moral Leadership: Getting to the Heart of School Improvement*, Jossey-Bass, San Francisco, 1992.
15 Available at http://www.smh.com.au/business/murdoch-lashes-abbott-on-journalists-law-20141023-11aryv.html#ixzz3H0ighoMR
16 Available at http://www.islamcan.com/islamic-stories/the-emperor-and-the-seed.shtml or http://www.anglicanyouth.org.nz/resources/talks/the-emperors-seeds
17 McGahey, V. T., 'Establishing Moral Community in Schools: Sensing the Spirit of School Leadership'; McGahey, V. T., 'Establishing Moral Community: Sensing the Spirit.'

Chapter 5

1   McGahey, V. T., 'Establishing Moral Community in Schools: Sensing the Spirit of School Leadership,' *Leading and Managing Journal*, 2002:8(1), pp. 60–77; McGahey, V. T., 'Establishing Moral Community: Sensing the Spirit,' unpublished doctoral dissertation, University of Western Sydney, Sydney, Australia, 2001.
2   Covey, S. R., *The 7 Habits of Highly Effective People: Powerful Lessons in Personal Change*, Fireside, New York, 1990, p. 178.
3   Anderson, L., *They Smell Like Sheep: Spiritual Leadership for the 21st Century*, Howard Books, West Monroe, Louisiana, 1997; McCormick, B. & Davenport, D., *Shepherd Leadership: Wisdom for Leaders from Psalm 23*, Jossey-Bass, San Francisco, 2003; McGahey, V. T., 'School Leadership for Establishing a Moral Community: The Shepherd Metaphor,' *Leading and Managing Journal*, 2000:6(1), pp. 77–94.
4   Gardner, H., *Leading Minds: An Anatomy of Leadership*, Basic Books, New York, 1995, p. 199; Notable Quotes: http://www.notable-quotes.com/r/roosevelt_eleanor.html
5   Available at http://www.americanrhetoric.com/speeches/eleanorroosevelt.htm
6   Available at http://www.un.org/en/globalissues/briefingpapers/humanrights/quotes.shtml

7   Numerous quote sites, such as: http://www.goodreads.com/quotes/6358-the-future-belongs-to-those-who-believe-in-the-beauty
8   McGahey, V. T., 'Establishing Moral Community in Schools: Sensing the Spirit of School Leadership'; McGahey, V. T., 'Establishing Moral Community: Sensing the Spirit.'
9   Bennis, W. & Nanus, B., *Leaders: The Strategies for Taking Charge*, Harper & Row, New York, 1985, p. 101.
10 Wenniger, M., 'Learning to Lead with Soul,' *Women in Higher Education*, 1997:6(7), p. 35.
11 Carnegie, D., *How To Win Friends & Influence People*, Angus & Robertson Publishers Pty Limited, Sydney, 1991, p. 223.
12 Transcript available at: http://www.ted.com/talks/ken_robinson_says_schools_kill_creativity/transcript?language=en
13 Maasen, S. & Weingart, P., *Metaphor and the Dynamics of Knowledge*, Routledge, London, 2000.
14 Bennis, W. & Nanus, B., *Leaders: The Strategies for Taking Charge*.
15 Crossan, M., Vera, D. & Nanjad, L., 'Transcendent Leadership: Strategic Leadership in Dynamic Environments,' *The Leadership Quarterly*, 2008:19(5), pp. 569–581.
16 Michie, S. & Gooty, J., 'Values, Emotions, and Authenticity: Will the Real Leader Please Stand Up?,' *The Leadership Quarterly*, 2005:16(3), pp. 441–457.
17 Estés, C. P., *Women Who Run With the Wolves*, Ballantine Books, New York, 1992, p. 32.
18 McGahey, V. T., 'Establishing Moral Community in Schools: Sensing the Spirit of School Leadership'; McGahey, V. T., 'Establishing Moral Community: Sensing the Spirit.'
19 Available at http://epistle.us/inspiration/godwillsaveme.html
20 Dreher, D., *Your Personal Renaissance: 12 Steps to Finding Your Life's True Calling*, Da Capo Press, Cambridge, Massachusetts, 2009.

Chapter 6

1   Lucia, A., 'Leaders Know How to Listen,' *HR Focus*, 1997:74, p. 25.
2   Carnegie, D., *How to Win Friends & Influence People*, Angus & Robertson Publishers Pty Limited, Sydney, 1991, pp. 38–40.
3   Available at http://www.goodreads.com/quotes/108466-judge-not-that-ye-be-not-judged
4   Goodwin, D. K., *Team Of Rivals: The Political Genius Of Abraham Lincoln*, Penguin, eBook, 2009.
5   Tzu, S., *The Art of War*, e-artnow, Prague, 2012.
6   McGahey, V. T., 'Establishing Moral Community in Schools: Sensing the Spirit of School Leadership,' *Leading and Managing Journal*, 2002:8(1), pp. 60–77; McGahey, V. T., 'Establishing Moral Community: Sensing the Spirit,' unpublished doctoral dissertation, University of Western Sydney, Sydney, Australia, 2001.
7   ibid.
8   Available at http://adb.anu.edu.au/biography/cowan-edith-dircksey-5791; http://www.australiangeographic.com.au/blogs/on-this-day/2011/08/on-this-day-australias-first-female-politician-born/

Endnotes

9. Covey, S. R., *The 7 Habits of Highly Effective People: Powerful Lessons in Personal Change*, Fireside, New York, 1990.
10. Gardiner, P. and Brien, K., *Mary MacKillop: An Extraordinary Australian*, Hear A Book, North Hobart, 1995. Available at: http://www.marymackillop.org.au/legacy/dsp-default.cfm?loadref=150
11. McGahey, V. T., 'Establishing Moral Community in Schools: Sensing the Spirit of School Leadership'; McGahey, V. T., 'Establishing Moral Community: Sensing the Spirit.'
12. Dreher, D., *The Tao of Personal Leadership: The Ancient Way to Success*, Thorsons, London, 1997.
13. Greene, R., *Mastery*, Penguin, London, 2012, pp. 50–54.
14. Darwin, C. & King-Hele, D., *Charles Darwin's The Life of Erasmus Darwin*, Cambridge University Press, Cambridge, England, 2003.
15. McGahey, V. T., 'Establishing Moral Community in Schools: Sensing the Spirit of School Leadership'; McGahey, V. T., 'Establishing Moral Community: Sensing the Spirit.'
16. Lama, D., *The Art of Happiness: A Handbook for Living*, Hodder Headline, Sydney, 2000.
17. Greene, R., *Mastery*, pp. 50–54.
18. Available at: http://www.royalgazette.com/article/20130212/COLUMN21/702129995; see also http://www.juliapittcoaching.com/.

Chapter 7

1. Available at http://quoteinvestigator.com/2013/01/01/einstein-imagination/; and for detail: https://www.psychologytoday.com/blog/imagine/201003/einstein-creative-thinking-music-and-the-intuitive-art-scientific-imagination
2. Wagmeister, J. & Shifrin, B., 'Thinking Differently, Learning Differently,' *Educational Leadership*, 2000:58(3), pp. 45–48.
3. Schön, D. A., 'Leadership as Reflection-in-Action,' in Sergiovanni, T. J. & Corbally, J. E. (eds.), *Leadership and Organizational Culture*, University of Illinois Press, Urbana, Illinois, 1984.
4. Reference source is Intuition Journal: http://intuitionjournal.com/blog/how-to-use-questions-to-access-your-intuition/
5. Greene, R., *Mastery*, Penguin, London, 2012, p. 266.
6. Available at https://cosmosmagazine.com/technology/ada-lovelace-prophet-computer-age; Ada Lovelace at biography.com website (retrieved from http://www.biography.com/people/ada-lovelace-20825323); and Bowden, B. V., 'Faster than Thought: A Symposium on Digital Computing Machines,' *The British Journal of Statistical Psychology*, 1955:8(1), pp. 59–64.
7. Greene, R., *Mastery*.
8. McGahey, V. T., 'Establishing Moral Community in Schools: Sensing the Spirit of School Leadership,' *Leading and Managing Journal*, 2002:8(1), pp. 60–77; McGahey, V. T., 'Establishing Moral Community: Sensing the Spirit,' unpublished doctoral dissertation, University of Western Sydney, Sydney, Australia, 2001.
9. Greenfield, T. & Ribbins, P., *Greenfield on Educational Administration: Towards a Humane Science*, Routledge, London and New York, 1993; Shelton, C., 'How to Use Intuition

to Build a Whole-Brained Organisation,' *Women in Higher Education*, 1997:6(8), p. 7; Starratt, R. J., *The Drama of Leadership*, Falmer Press, London, 1993; Starratt, R. J., *Transforming Educational Administration: Meaning, Community, and Excellence*, McGraw-Hill, New York, 1996; Wenniger, M., 'Learning to Lead with Soul,' *Women in Higher Education*, 1997:6(7), p. 8; Westerhof, C., 'Let Intuition Guide Your Decision Making on Campus,' *Women in Higher Education*, 1997:6(19), p. 27.

10 Wenniger, M., 'Learning to Lead with Soul.'
11 Available at: http://hca.gilead.org.il/ugly_duc.html
12 McGahey, V. T., 'Establishing Moral Community in Schools: Sensing the Spirit of School Leadership.'
13 Eknath Easwaren, *Gandhi The Man,* in Dreher, D., *The Tao of Personal Leadership: The Ancient Way to Success*, Thorsons, London, 1997, p. 209.
14 Available at http://events.nationalgeographic.com/speakers-bureau/speaker/sylvia-earle/; http://www.nationalgeographic.com.explorers.bios/sylvia-earle and http://www.achievement.org/autodoc/page/ear0bio-1
15 McGahey, V. T., 'Establishing Moral Community in Schools: Sensing the Spirit of School Leadership'; McGahey, V. T., 'Establishing Moral Community: Sensing the Spirit.'
16 Available at http://lifereimagined.aarp.org/stories/4911-The-Art-of-Taking-Risks
17 Available at http://www.rozsavage.com/
18 Available at http://www.diananyad.com/diana

Chapter 8

1 Dreher, D., *The Tao of Personal Leadership: The Ancient Way to Success*, Thorsons, London, 1997, p. 208.
2 McGahey, V. T., 'The Most Important Learners In School Are Not The Students,' *REFLECT Journal*, 1997:3(1), pp. 6–13, p. 7.
3 Dewey, J., *How We Think: A Restatement of the Relation of Reflective Thinking to the Educative Process*, D. C. Heath & Co., Boston, 1933.
4 Goleman, D., *Emotional Intelligence: Why It Can Matter More Than IQ*, Bloomsbury, London, 1995.
5 Killion, J. P. & Todnem, G. R., 'A Process for Personal Theory Building,' *Educational Leadership*, 1991:48(6), pp. 14–16, p. 14.
6 Available at http://talilandsmanart.com/2014/03/21/grace-is-hidden-behind-misfortune-suspend-judgement-until-you-gain-a-wider-perspective/
7 McGahey, V. T., 'Establishing Moral Community in Schools: Sensing the Spirit of School Leadership,' *Leading and Managing Journal*, 2002:8(1), pp. 60–77; McGahey, V. T., 'Establishing Moral Community: Sensing the Spirit,' unpublished doctoral dissertation, University of Western Sydney, Sydney, Australia.
8 Available at http://talilandsmanart.com/2014/03/21/grace-is-hidden-behind-misfortune-suspend-judgement-until-you-gain-a-wider-perspective/
9 Available at http://archive.wired.com/science/planetearth/magazine/15-09/ff_lagoon?currentPage=all

10 Available at http://www.hcamag.com/hr-news/2015-year-of-the-diverse-workforce-195467.aspx

11 ibid.

12 Available at http://www.hcamag.com/hr-resources/diversity/

13 Beatty, B., *A Treasury of Australian Folklore*, Lifetime Distributors, Sydney, 1960.

14 McGahey, V. T., 'Establishing Moral Community in Schools: Sensing the Spirit of School Leadership'; McGahey, V. T., 'Establishing Moral Community: Sensing the Spirit.'

15 McGahey, V. T., 'Establishing Moral Community in Schools: Sensing the Spirit of School Leadership.'

16 Available at http://skdesigns.com/internet/articles/quotes/williamson/our_deepest_fear/

Chapter 9

1 Church, M., *Amplifiers: The Power of Motivational Leadership to Inspire and Influence*, John Wiley & Sons, Milton, Queensland, 2013, p. 102.

2 Lucia, A., 'Leaders Know How to Listen,' *HR Focus*, 1997:74, p. 25.

3 Anderson, L., *They Smell Like Sheep: Spiritual Leadership for The 21st Century*, Howard Books, West Monroe, Louisiana, 1997; Roper, D., The Lord Is My Shepherd [Online], 1995. (Retrieved from http://www2.gospelcom.net/Rbc/Ds/Hp952/Hp952/html/ [1999, Nov 10], and available at https://d3uet6ae1sqvww.cloudfront.net/pdf/discovery-series/the-lord-is-my-shepherd.pdf.); Laniak, T. S., *Shepherds After My Own Heart: Pastoral Traditions And Leadership In The Bible*, InterVarsity Press, Downers Grove, Illinois, 2006; McCormick, B. & Davenport, D., *Shepherd Leadership: Wisdom for Leaders from Psalm 23*, Jossey-Bass, San Francisco, 2003; McGahey, V. T., 'School Leadership for Establishing a Moral Community: The Shepherd Metaphor,' *Leading and Managing Journal*, 2000:6(1), pp. 77–94.

4 Remen, R. N., *Kitchen Table Wisdom: Stories That Heal*, Pan Macmillan Australia, Sydney, Australia, 2002.

5 McGahey, V. T., 'Establishing Moral Community in Schools: Sensing the Spirit of School Leadership' *Leading and Managing Journal*, 2002:8(1), pp. 60–77; McGahey, V. T., 'Establishing Moral Community: Sensing the Spirit,' unpublished doctoral dissertation, University of Western Sydney, Sydney, Australia, 2001.

6 Available at https://www.goodreads.com/quotes/152272-the-most-basic-and-powerful-way-to-connect-to-another

7 McGahey, V. T., 'Establishing Moral Community in Schools: Sensing the Spirit of School Leadership'; McGahey, V. T., 'Establishing Moral Community: Sensing the Spirit.'

8 Available at http://blog.professionalcc.com/2012/04/23/trench-leadership/

9 Available at http://www.cs.yale.edu/homes/tap/Files/hopper-story.html

10 Available at http://www.directcreative.com/influence-and-persuasion-the-rule-of-consistency.html

11 Based on Aesop's fable, *The Hare and the Tortoise*. Available at http://www.aesopfables.com/

12 McGahey, V. T., 'Establishing Moral Community in Schools: Sensing the Spirit of School Leadership'; McGahey, V. T., 'Establishing Moral Community: Sensing the Spirit.'

13 Based on Aesop's fable, *The Scorpion and the Frog*. Available at http://www.aesopfables.com/

Chapter 10

1 Dreher, D., *The Tao of Personal Leadership: The Ancient Way to Success*, Thorsons, London, 1997, p. 246.

2 Dreher, D., *The Tao of Personal Leadership: The Ancient Way to Success*, p. 138.

3 Bowling, J. C., *Grace-Full Leadership: Understanding the Heart of a Christian Leader*, Beacon Hill Press, Kansas City, 2011; McGahey, V. T., 'School Leadership for Establishing a Moral Community: The Shepherd Metaphor,' *Leading and Managing Journal*, 2000:6(1), pp. 77–94.

4 Bowling, J. C., *Grace-Full Leadership: Understanding the Heart of a Christian Leader*; Gardner, H., *Frames Of Mind: The Theory of Multiple Intelligences*, Basic Books, New York, 1993; Goleman, D., *Emotional Intelligence: Why It Can Matter More Than IQ*, Bloomsbury, London, 1995; Goleman, D., *Working with Emotional Intelligence*, Bloomsbury, London, 1997.

5 Calhoun, E. F., 'Relationship Of Teachers' Conceptual Level To The Utilisation Of Supervisory Services And To A Description Of The Classroom Instructional Improvement,' paper presented at the Annual Meeting of the American Educational Research Association, Illinois, April 1985; Glickman, C. D., 'Developing Teacher Thought,' *Journal Of Staff Development*, 1986:7(1), pp. 6–21; Hunt, D. E. & Joyce, B. R., 'Teacher Trainee Personality And Teaching Style,' *American Educational Research Journal*, 1967:4, pp. 253–255.

6 Goleman, D., *Emotional Intelligence: Why It Can Matter More Than IQ*, p. 34.

7 Bredfeldt, G. J., *Great Leader, Great Teacher: Recovering the Biblical Vision for Leadership*, Moody Publishers, Chicago, 2006; Gow, K., 'What Are The Required Outcomes Of Education – Professional Competencies, Personal Attributes And Social Skills,' paper presented at the Queensland State Conference Of National Association Of Post Compulsory Educators, Surfers Paradise, Australia, 1997 (ERIC Document, Ed 407569); Lowney, C., *Heroic Leadership: Best Practices of a 450-Year-Old Company that Changed the World*, Loyola Press, Chicago, 2003.

8 Bowling, J. C., *Grace-Full Leadership: Understanding the Heart of a Christian Leader*; Bredfeldt, G. J., *Great Leader, Great Teacher: Recovering the Biblical Vision for Leadership*; Lowney, C., *Heroic Leadership: Best Practices of a 450-Year-Old Company that Changed the World*; McGahey, V. T., 'School Leadership for Establishing a Moral Community: The Shepherd Metaphor'; McGahey, V. T., 'Establishing Moral Community in Schools: Sensing the Spirit of School Leadership,' *Leading and Managing Journal*, 2002:8(1), pp. 60–77.

9 Carnes, P. G., 'Like Sheep Without A Shepherd: The Shepherd Metaphor and Its Primacy For Biblical Leadership,' doctoral dissertation, Reformed Theological Seminary, 2007; McCormick, B. & Davenport, D., *Shepherd Leadership: Wisdom for Leaders from Psalm 23*, Jossey-Bass, San Francisco, 2003.

10 Dreher, D., *The Tao of Personal Leadership: The Ancient Way to Success*, p. 231.

11 Anderson, L., *They Smell Like Sheep: Spiritual Leadership for the 21st Century*, Howard Books, West Monroe, Louisiana, 1997; Laniak, T. S., *Shepherds After My Own Heart: Pastoral Traditions And Leadership In The Bible*, InterVarsity Press, Downers Grove,

Illinois, 2006; McCormick, B. & Davenport, D., *Shepherd Leadership: Wisdom for Leaders from Psalm 23*; McGahey, V. T., 'School Leadership for Establishing a Moral Community: The Shepherd Metaphor.'

12. Roper, D., The Lord Is My Shepherd [Online], 1995. (Retrieved from http://Www2.Gospelcom.Net/Rbc/Ds/Hp952/Hp952/Html/ [1999, Nov 10], p.3, and available at https://d3uet6ae1sqvww.cloudfront.net/pdf/discovery-series/the-lord-is-my-shepherd.pdf.
13. Dreher, D., *The Tao of Personal Leadership: The Ancient Way to Success*, p. 131.
14. Larimer, L.V., 'Reflections on Ethics and Integrity,' *HR Focus*, 1997:74, p. 5.
15. Bowling, J. C., *Grace-Full Leadership: Understanding the Heart of a Christian Leader*, p. 20.
16. Cormode, S., 'Multi-Layered Leadership: The Christian Leader As Builder, Shepherd, And Gardener,' *Journal Of Religious Leadership*, 2002:(2), pp. 69–104, p. 82.

Index

13 Virtues of Benjamin Franklin, The
  (story) 40–41, 207

A

A Prophet of Hope (story) 77–78
A Story of Service (story) 45–46
A Treasury of Australian Folklore 147–148
A Wise Fable (story) 56
A Woman of Compassion (story)
  106–107
A Woman of Grace (story) 101–103
Alice of Battenberg, Princess 45–46
Andersen, Hans Christian 126–128
Archimedes, creativity of 120
Aristotle 82
authenticity, integrity in 57
awarenesses held by leaders 31–32

B

Babbage, Charles 123
Bacon, Francis 161
Bag of Gold, The – Shiva and Shakti
  (story) 41–42
Barna Group survey 44
Beatty, Bill 147–148
'becoming' 36–47
Beecher, Henry Ward 105
benefits of leading 32–33
Bennis, Warren 39
born leaders 21
Bowden, B.V. 124
Bowling, John C. 54
Boyd, D. 189
Bradbury, Ray 131
Bridge Crossing, The (story) 63–64
Bula! – The Fijian Connection (story)
  82–83
Burns, George 112
Butte, Montana 142–143

C

Camelot, legend of 11
Canfield, Jack 43–44
Carnegie, Dale 81, 97
Chaos Theory 82–83, 83
Chicken Soup for the Soul 43–44
chosen leaders 21

Chosen People, The (story) 89
Christian faith
  leadership and 40
  on risk 133
Church, Matt 153
Cleveland State University study 64
Collections (story) 113–114
communication, as Leadership Attribute
  152–167, 182–183
community building *see also* moral
  community
  challenging to take action 79–80
  conceptual theories 192–194
  with followers 31
compassion
  as Leadership Attribute 105–111, 181
  related to empathy 95, 104
conceptual theories, Leadership Attributes
  Study 186–196
Confederate Escape (story) 97–99
conflict, dealing with 59–60
Confucius 91
Connery, Sean 11
consistency
  as Leadership Attribute 161–167,
  183
  related to communication 152, 160
constructivism 189
convergent media 24
Covey, Stephen
  on compassion 105
  on diversity 145
  on leadership 76
  on trust 63
  on understanding 152
Cowan, Edith 100–103
creativity, need for 25
Credibility Through Honesty (story) 64
Curie, Marie 36

D

Dalai Lama 110, 115–116
Darwin, Charles 113–114
Declaration of Human Rights 77–78
Descartes, René 120
Dewey, John 138
Disraeli, Benjamin 161

Index

diversity
  as Leadership Attribute 145, 182
  related to judgment 137
domination, leadership by 20
dopamine 134
Dreher, Diane 93, 138, 169, 170, 172, 201
Duty Roster (story) 59

E

Earle, Dr Sylvia 131–132
Eason, Cassandra 63
ego, satisfying 30
Einstein, Albert
  creativity of 120
  on imagination 121
  on intuition 118
  on mystery 89
  on safety 130
Elizabeth II, Queen 39
emancipatory discourse 189
empathy, as Leadership Attribute 95–117, 181
Emperor's Seed, The (story) 71–72
essence of leadership 34
'Establishing Moral Community: Sensing the Spirit' 188, 193
Estés, Clarissa Pinkola 87–88
Ezekiel's Wheel 87–88

F

faith
  as Leadership Attribute 181
  prophecy and 75
  related to prophecy 91–94
Fiji, greetings in 82–83
followers, community building and 31
Four Rabbis, The (story) 87–88
Franklin, Benjamin
  13 virtues of 40–41, 207
  creativity of 120
  Intuitive Creations (story) 122–123
Freedom House index 70
Freire, Paulo 189
Frugal Innovation in Healthcare 191
fundamentalism, resisting 13

G

Gandhi, Mahatma
  Duty Roster (story) 59
  integrity of 56–57
  quote from 130

The Sugar Story (story) 60–61
gathering action 169–170, 200–201
gender issues
  gender imbalance in leadership 12–13, 23
  workplace discrimination 29
globalisation, needs developing from 22
God Will Save Me (story) 92
Golden Buddha, The (story) 43–44
Goleman, Daniel 138
Gonzalez, Ruben 59
Good Samaritan parable 199
grace, being in 31
Granny Smith Apple (story) 147–148
Greene, Robert 113–114, 124

H

Hansen, Mark Victor 43–44
Hemingway, Ernest 63, 152
higher ideals, leadership by 20
Hitler, Adolf 115
Holy Spirit 39–40
Hopper, Grace 158–159
How to Win Friends & Influence People 81
human rights 22–23

I

Inner Wheel (Rotary) 88
innovation, need for 25
Institute of the Sisters of St Joseph 19
integrity, as Leadership Attribute 54–74, 180
intuition, as Leadership Attribute 118–136, 182
Intuitive Creations (story) 122–123
Invitation, The (poem) 27–28, 204–206
Isurava memorial 110
It Comes From the Heart (story) 38–39

J

judgment, as Leadership Attribute 137–151, 182
Just Listen (story) 154

K

Kane, Sue and Leo 19
Kangaroo and the Echidna, The (story) 162–163
Keith Murdoch Oration (story) 69–70
Keller, Helen 130
Kennedy, John F. 85

King, Martin Luther Jr 85
Kitchen Table Wisdom 41–42
'knowing', the 28, 86
Kokoda track 110

L

Landsman, Tali 140, 142
Lao Tzu 112, 172
leadership
  conceptual theories 190–192
  defined 31–32
  integrity valued in 56–57
  origins of 18–35
  power and 30
  promoting women in 29
  women under-represented in 23
Leadership Attributes
  descriptions of 14–15
  in action 168–174
  list of 180–183
  making use of 33
  model of 50–53
Leadership Attributes Study, conceptual theories 186–196
leadership teams 32
learning, transformative 12, 187–190
Lincoln, Abraham
  empathy of 97–99
  integrity of 55
  quotes from 107, 139
Listen! Really Listen (story) 155
Little Brown Book, The 19
Lorenz, Edward 83
Lost Sheep parable 199
Lovelace, Ada 120, 123–124, 159
Lucia, Alexander 96

M

MacDonald, George 68
McGahey, Vicky
  jungle trip by 108–110
  The Voice Within (story) 119
McKee, M. H. 54
MacKillop, Mary
  and the Pub (story) 19
  compassion of 106–107
  quotes from 105, 137
Mary MacKillop and the Pub (story) 19
Mastery 124
Match Point (story) 59
Menabrea, Luigi Federico 123

messages, buying into 26
Meyer, J. Gordon 189
Mezirow, Jack 187
Microscopic World, The (story) 116
Mill, The (story) 81
model of Leadership Attributes 50–53
Modelling (story) 158
modelling, integrity in 57
moral community *see also* community building
  defined 12
  empathy in 100
  integrity in 58
More Risk Taking (story) 135
mottos
  be prepared to make a stand 75
  be still and listen 152
  'become' yourself 54
  listen to feel 95
  suspend judgment; accept diversity and change 137
  the perception of truth 118
Mount Remarkable, SA 19
Mozart, Wolfgang, creativity of 120
Mt Remarkable, SA 19
Murdoch Keith 69–70
Murdoch, Lachlan 69–70
Mutualism and Suspending Judgment – The Cuckoo (story) 140
MV *Orient Express* 11
My Life is My Message (story) 56–57

N

Newton, Isaac 120
Nyad, Diana 135

O

Old Lady and the Hearing Aid, The (story) 65–66
One of Life's More Memorable Experiences (story) 108–110
Oriah Mountain Dreamer 27–28, 204–206

P

Parable of the Pencil, The (story) 36–37
Parable of the Talents, The (story) 132–133
passion
  as Leadership Attribute 112–117, 181
  related to empathy 95

Index

pathfinding action 170–172, 200
Patten, E. J. 91
Pencil, The Parable of the (story) 36–37
Pierce, William 123
Pitt, Julia 116
presence action 172–173, 199–200
procrastination 142
Prodigal Son parable 199
prophecy, as Leadership Attribute 75–94, 181
Prophet of Hope, A (story) 77–78
Prophet of the Computer Age, The (story) 123–124

R

Read, Jenny 50, 197
reflective action
 on communication 160
 on compassion 111
 on consistency 167
 on diversity 151
 on empathy 104
 on faith 94
 on integrity 62
 on intuition 129
 on judgment 144
 on Leadership Attributes 179
 on passion 117
 on prophecy 84
 on risk 136
 on transcendence 90
 on trust 62
 on trustworthiness 73
 suspending judgement for 138–139
relationships, integrity in 57–58
Remen, Rachel Naomi
 Just Listen (story) 154
 quotes from 95, 155
 The Bag of Gold – Shiva and Shakti (story) 41–42
risk
 as Leadership Attribute 130, 182
 related to intuition 118
Risk Taking (story) 134–135
Robinson, Mary, on world poverty 39
Robinson, Sir Ken 82
Roosevelt, Eleanor
 A Prophet of Hope (story) 77–78
 quotes from 22–23, 75
Roosevelt, Franklin D., on leadership 31
Rotary International 82, 88

S

Sacrifice and Suspending Judgment –
 The Snow Geese (story) 142–143
Saint Joseph, Sisters of 19
Savage, Roz 134–135
Schwab, Charles H. 81
Scorpion and the Platypus, The (story) 164–165
service
 leadership as 32
 learning through 44–45
Shaw, George Bernard 112
Shepherd Metaphor of leadership 34, 153, 168–169, 197–203
Sisters of St Joseph 19
Small, E. H. 148
Smurfs, The, story from 38–39
soul, venturing into 44
Specialist Music School 11–12
spirit, sensing 31–32
St Joseph, Sisters of 19
stories and poems
 A Prophet of Hope 77–78
 A Story of Service 45–46
 A Wise Fable 56
 A Woman of Compassion 106–107
 A Woman of Grace 101–103
 Bula! – The Fijian Connection 82–83
 Collections 113–114
 Confederate Escape 97–99
 Credibility Through Honesty 64
 Duty Roster 59
 God Will Save Me 92
 Granny Smith Apple 147–148
 Intuitive Creations 122–123
 It Comes From the Heart 38–39
 Just Listen 154
 Keith Murdoch Oration 69–70
 Listen! Really Listen 155
 Mary MacKillop and the Pub 19
 Match Point 59
 Modelling 158
 More Risk Taking 135
 Mutualism and Suspending Judgment –
  The Cuckoo 140
 My Life is My Message 56–57
 One of Life's More Memorable
  Experiences 108–110
 Risk Taking 134–135
 Sacrifice and Suspending Judgment –
  The Snow Geese 142–143

Taking Risks 131–132
The 13 Virtues of Benjamin Franklin 40–41
The Bag of Gold – Shiva and Shakti 41–42
The Bridge Crossing 63–64
The Chosen People 89
The Emperor's Seed 71–72
The Four Rabbis 87–88
The Invitation 204–206
The Kangaroo and the Echidna 162–163
The Microscopic World 116
The Mill 81
The Old Lady and the Hearing Aid 65–66
The Parable of the Pencil 36–37
The Parable of the Talents 132–133
The Prophet of the Computer Age 123–124
The Scorpion and the Platypus 164–165
The Sugar Story 60–61
The Ugly Duckling 126
The Voice Within 119
Wise Use of Analogies 158–159
Words of Insight 149–150
succession planning, importance of 32
Sugar Story, The (story) 60–61
Sun Tzu 99
symbols
  heart 95
  key 75
  pen and voice 152
  scale 137
  soul and rainbow 118
  yin and yang 54

T

Taking Risks (story) 131–132
Talents, The Parable of the (story) 132-133
Tao Te Ching
  on gathering 169
  on judgment 138
  on leadership 201
  on presence 172
technological change 24
'the knowing' 28, 86

The… (stories and poems) *see under second word of title*
transcendence
  as Leadership Attribute 181
  prophecy and 75
  related to prophecy 84–90
'Transcendent Leadership: Strategic Leadership in Dynamic Environments' 85
transformative leadership 12
transformative learning 12, 187–190
Treasury of Australian Folklore, A 147–148
trust
  as Leadership Attribute 180
  related to integrity 62, 63–67
trustworthy/trustworthiness
  as Leadership Attribute 180
  related to integrity 62, 68–73

U

Ugly Duckling, The (story) 126–128

V

van Leeuwenhoek, Antonie 116
vision, collective 86
Voice Within, The (story) 119

W

Whitman, Walt 137
Williamson, Marianne 149–150
Wise Fable, A (story) 56
Wise Use of Analogies (story) 158–159
Woman of Compassion, A (story) 106–107
Woman of Grace, A (story) 101–103
women in leadership 12–13, 29 *see also* gender issues
Women Who Run With the Wolves 87–88
Women's Legal Status Bill 101
Woods, Julian Tenison 19, 106–107
Words of Insight (story) 149–150
workplace discrimination against women 29
world leaders, failure of 24–25

Y

Your Personal Renaissance 93
Yousafzai, Malala 21

Additional information

The Leadership Attributes have evolved into a number of new and different ways of learning for people of all ages. The following products are available through my website: www.vickymcgahey.com:

1. The Leadership Attributes Journal: intended as a companion to this book, this free journal has been created for you to use as you reflect upon these attributes and the work within this book.
2. The Leadership Attributes Game: a card game based upon the leadership attributes. Designed to encourage dialogue and participation and suitable for all ages.
3. Leadership Attributes Cards of Reflection: a new tool designed to help focus the mind, heart and soul on each of the attributes; a problem-solving tool with strategies to help to reveal inner thoughts and solve problems.
4. Young Adult series of books – *The Kingdom of Wizards*.

Visit Vicky's website to download your **free journal** to record your thoughts and reflections as you read this book (the journal includes mandalas to colour in).

www.vickymcgahey.com